ENABLING
AND
EMPOWERING
FAMILIES

ENABLING AND EMPOWERING FAMILIES

Principles and Guidelines for Practice

Carl J. Dunst
Carol M. Trivette
Angela G. Deal

With Contributions From:

Pat Bell
Joyce Chase
P.J. Cushing
Nancy Gordon
R.A. McWilliam
Donald Mott
Lynda Pletcher

Lynne Sharpe
Tina Swanson
Sherra Vance
Bonnie Walker
Janet Weeldreyer
Linda Wilson
Linda Wortman Lowe

BROOKLINE BOOKS
Cambridge, MA

Library of Congress Cataloging-in-Publication Data

Dunst, Carl J.
    Enabling and empowering families.

    Bibliography: p.
    Includes index.
    1. Handicapped children—Home care—United States.
2. Handicapped children—United States—Family
relationships. 3. Family social work—United States.
I. Trivette, Carol M. II. Deal, Angela G. III. Title.
HV888.5.D86 1988   362.4'088054   87–27851
ISBN 0–914797–44–1

Published by
Brookline Books, Inc.
PO Box 1046
Cambridge, MA 02238–1046

Printed in the United States of America at McNaughton and Gunn, Inc.

Dedication

To all of the families that we have had the opportunity to know and learn from and who have taught us that the best way to be of help is to support and strengthen family functioning.

Contents

Preface

The principles and guidelines for enabling and empowering families described in this book have evolved from seven years of research and clinical work at the Western Carolina Center Family, Infant and Preschool Program in Morganton, North Carolina. This work has included both the conduct of numerous empirical investigations designed to disentangle the complexities of family functioning and a series of model-demonstration projects that have developed, field-tested, and validated different approaches for helping families identify and meet their needs in a way that strengthens family functioning. The material described in this book represents the aggregate of this research and clinical work. It is designed specifically for use by professionals working in the early intervention field, although the procedures have utility for other helping professionals.

Early intervention practitioners are increasingly asked to function as ''family specialists'' in their work with handicapped and at-risk children. This shift in role emphasis has occurred, in part, as a result of the recognition that the child is a member of a family system and that events both within and outside the family unit impinge upon the success of early intervention efforts. Indeed, it is now safe to say that early intervention programs that employ a broader-based, family systems approach will likely have positive influences on all family members, whereas traditional, child-focused intervention practices will produce meager results at best. The shift in role emphasis we are witnessing in the field of early intervention is perhaps most apparent in light of recent federal legislation. The Reauthorization of the Education for All Handicapped Children Act (Public Law 99–457) specifically requires the preschool intervention programs use a family systems model as part of early intervention practices with handicapped infants and toddlers and their families.

Although we are asking early intervention professionals to take on expanded roles in their work with handicapped and at-risk children and their families, at least one major problem remains. Many if not most early intervention practitioners have had little or no training in work with families. This state of affairs has created considerable controversy. On the one hand there are those who believe that early intervention practitioners, particularly those who have been trained as child therapists or infant educators, should not delve into family issues because they lack the proper knowledge and skills to understand or engage in family systems intervention. On the other hand there are those, including ourselves, who believe that anyone who works with a child in an early intervention program will influence the family system, intentionally or not, and is likely to have positive or negative effects on the family unit depending upon the manner in which assessments and interventions are conducted. Because of this, we believe that early intervention practitioners need to be knowledgeable and skilled so that they can intervene in ways that have positive rather than negative consequences.

This book was specifically written for early intervention practitioners who are being asked to work with families but who have not had extensive training in family systems assessment and intervention procedures. We have taken very complex material regarding social and family systems theory and have reduced it to a set of four principles that can be used to meet the needs of family members in a way that increases the likelihood that interventions will have positive effects on child, parent, and family functioning. The principles are derived from research evidence and clinical experience that suggest the most efficacious ways in which assessments and interventions ought to be conducted. Each principle has a number of operatives that guide the ways in which the principle is put into practice. Collectively, the principles and operatives represent a framework and set of guidelines for promoting a family's ability to identify its needs and mobilize resources in a way that strengthens family functioning.

As the title of our book reflects, the notions of enablement and empowerment are fundamental to our approach to working with families. By "enablement," we mean creating opportunities for *ALL* family members to display and acquire competencies that strengthen family functioning. The first theme of our book, and one that diverges from common intervention practices, is the focus on the family—and not an individual family member—as the unit of intervention. By "empowerment," we mean a family's ability to meet needs and achieve aspirations in a way that promotes a clear sense of intrafamily mastery and control over important aspects of family functioning. A second theme that permeates our approach to working with families is the contention that it is not simply a matter of whether or not family needs are met that should be used to judge the success of intervention efforts. Unless needs are met in a way that makes the family more competent with respect to its ability to negotiate its course of development, the opportunity to strengthen family functioning will be lost.

A third theme of our book is the all-important belief (some would say obsession) that parents have the rightful role in deciding what is important for themselves and their family, and that the family and the family alone bears the responsibility for deciding its course of development—to the extent that the well-being and rights of all family members are protected. The role of a professional *must* be to support and strengthen the family's ability to nurture and promote the development of its members in a way that is both enabling and empowering.

A fourth theme, albeit a minor one, also deserves comment since it underscores our approach to working with families. Early intervention practitioners often assume a "poor, unfortunate creature" and a "gloom-and-doom" stance toward families of disadvantaged and handicapped children, respectively. The former often results in well-intentioned individuals giving and mobilizing resources on behalf of families where individual family members play little or no active role in accessing the resources. The latter often results in focusing on the negative aspects of the child and his or her adverse impacts on the family unit, sometimes to the point that we search for things that "must be" wrong despite the fact that the family has adapted and is functioning well. It is a maxim of our approach to working with families that one must *see* the positive, *focus* on the positive, and *promote* positive functioning as the major emphasis of the intervention process.

Our book is divided into eight chapters. First, we introduce the reader to a number of social systems concepts and present eight maxims—beliefs and principles—that form the basis of our model. Second, we discuss the meaning of need and illustrate the ways in which needs influence behavior. Third, we describe the differences between intrafamily and extrafamily resources and examine how those resources are used by families to meet their individualized needs. Fourth, we summarize what is known about helping relationships and how different "helping styles" have different effects on individual and family functioning. Fifth, we propose a minimal set of intervention principles that permit translation of both theory and research into practice. Sixth, we describe the operation of a needs-based assessment and intervention model. Seventh, we present a number of case studies that illustrate the application and utility of the assessment and intervention model. We conclude by describing the necessity for a "fluid" conceptualization of family-level intervention plans as part of the development of the Individualized Family Service Plan required by the newly established Early Intervention Program as part of P.L. 99–457 (Part H). Collectively, the material presented in the various chapters represents both a conceptual and programmatic framework for helping families identify and meet their needs in a way that is both enabling and empowering. We hope users of our family systems assessment and intervention model find the material presented in this book helpful in improving their ability to work effectively with families participating in early intervention programs.

Acknowledgments

The completion of this book would not have been possible without the help of many friends and colleagues. First and foremost, we would like to extend special thanks to all of the staff of the Family, Infant and Preschool Program and the many families who participated in the various phases of the development and validation of the model described in this book. We would like to acknowledge, with much gratitude, Faith Bolick, Kim Galant, Patti Gilbert, Nancy Gordon, Hope Leet, Robin McWilliam, Lynda Pletcher, Janet Weeldreyer, and Sherra Vance, staff of the projects who field-tested different ways of enabling and empowering families. Pat Condrey and Norma Hunter typed numerous versions of this book, and their patience and assistance are greatly appreciated. Thanks is also extended to Pam Lowman and Olivia Carswell for typing different versions of the case study material. The graphics, artwork, and reference materials were completed by Michael Baker, Wilson Hamer, Wendy Jodry, Peggy Mankinen, and Debra Smith, and computer assistance was provided by Wayne deLoriea. Their help and assistance are appreciated as well. Lastly, special thanks and recognition are extended to Iverson Riddle, M.D., Director, Western Carolina Center, for his continued support and encouragement throughout the process of developing and implementing the methods and procedures for enabling and empowering families described in this book.

The research described herein was supported, in part, by grants from the National Institute of Mental Health, Prevention Research Branch (MH38862), and the North Carolina Department of Human Resources, Research and Evaluation Section (83527). The model-demonstration projects that served as the arena for development and field-testing of various versions of the assessment and intervention model were supported, in part, by grants from the U.S. Department of Health and Human Services, Administration on Developmental Disabilities (90DD0113), the U.S. Department of Education, Office of Special Education Programs (GOO8530078), the North Carolina State Board of Education, Children's Trust Fund (C7753), and the North Carolina Council on Developmental Disabilities.

We would also like to thank the following authors and publishers for permission to reprint material in this book:

American Psychological Association, Washington, DC, for permission to reprint material from Bandura, A., "Self-efficacy: Toward a unifying theory of behavioral change." *Psychological Review*, 1977, *84*, pp. 191–215.

Brunner/Mazel, Inc., New York, NY, for permission to reprint material from Bronfenbrenner, U., "Is early intervention effective?" In B. Friedlander, G. Sterritt, & G. Kirk (Eds.), *Exceptional Infant: Vol. 3. Assessment and intervention*, 1975, pp. 465–466.

Aldine de Gruyter, Hawthorne, NY, and to James Garbarino, for permission to reprint material from Garbarino, J. *Children and families in the social environment*, pp. 13, 72. Copyright (c) 1982 by James Garbarino.

Department of Human Development and the Family, Center for Family Strengths, University of Nebraska, Lincoln, NE, for permission to reprint material from Williams, R., Lindgren, H., Rowe, G., Van Zandt, S., Lee, P., & Stinnett, N. (Eds.), *Family strengths 6: Enhancement of interaction*, Preface, 1985.

Family Process Press, Syracuse, NY, for permission to reprint material from Otto, H., "Criteria for assessing family strengths." *Family Process*, 2(2), 1963, p. 329.

Harvard University Press, Cambridge, MA, for permission to reprint material from Bronfenbrenner, U., *The ecology of human development: Experiments by nature and design*, 1979, p. 7.

Herbert A. Otto for permission to reprint material from *The use of family strength concepts and methods in family life education: A handbook*, 1975, p. 16.

Jossey-Bass, Inc., Publishers, San Francisco, CA, for permission to reprint material from Hobbs, N., Dokecki, P.R., Hoover-Dempsey, K.V., Moroney, R.M., Shayne, M.W., & Weeks, K.H., *Strengthening families*, 1984, p. 45.

Pergamon Press, Inc., Elmsford, NY, and to Carl J. Dunst for permission to reprint material from "Rethinking early intervention." *Analysis and Intervention in Developmental Disabilities*, 5, p. 171. Copyright (c) 1985 by Pergamon Press Ltd.

Plenum Publishing Corporation, New York, NY, and to Julian Rappaport for permission to reprint material from "In praise of paradox: A social policy of empowerment over prevention." *American Journal of Community Psychology*, 1981, 9(1), pp. 16–17.

Sage Publications, Inc., Newbury Park, CA, and to Frank F. Maple for permission to reprint material from *Shared decision making*, pp. 7, 54. Copyright (c) 1977 by Sage Publications, Inc.

Sage Publications, Inc., Newbury Park, CA, and to Benjamin H. Gottlieb for permission to reprint material from *Social support strategies: Guidelines for mental health practice*, p. 210. Copyright (c) 1983 by Sage Publications, Inc.

University Press of New England, Hanover, NH, for permission to reprint material from Pilisuk, M., & Parks, S.H., *The healing web: Social networks and human survival*, pp. 162–163. Copyright (c) 1986 by University Press of New England.

1
Introduction

Over a decade ago, Bronfenbrenner (1975) made the following claim:

> ... intervention programs that place major emphasis on involving the parent *directly* in activities fostering the child's development are likely to have constructive impact at any age, but the earlier such activities are begun, and the longer they are continued, the greater the benefit to the child. (p. 465)

This assertion is often included in efforts to justify parent involvement in early intervention programs. It is unfortunate, however, that those who cite Bronfenbrenner as a basis for arguing that parent involvement is crucial to the success of early intervention do not take into consideration the conditions he described in his next paragraph. He went on to state:

> One major problem still remains. ... [Many] families live under such oppressive circumstances that they are neither willing nor able to participate in the activities required by a parent intervention program. Inadequate health care, poor housing, lack of education, low income and the necessity for full-time work ... *rob parents of time and energy* [italics added] to spend with their children. (pp. 465–466)

In the decade since Bronfenbrenner noted the adverse conditions that are likely to interfere with parents having the time and energy to be directly involved in early intervention programs, we have seen a dramatic change in one particular condition that is likely to impinge upon the ability of parents to be directly involved in their children's early education—namely, the need or desire for mothers to work outside the home. According to recent U.S. Department of Labor (1987) statistics, 34% of all mothers of children younger than three years of age were in the labor force in 1975. In 1986, the figure had risen to 51%. Similar changes are evident for mothers of 3- to 5-year-old children. In 1975, 45% of mothers of children of this age range were in the work force, compared to 60% in 1986. If this trend continues, as appears will be the case, by the year 2000 over 75% of all mothers of children under age six will be working outside the home. This cannot but become an even more important reason why parents may not have the time and energy to be directly involved in early intervention programs, at least in the way family involvement has traditionally been conceptualized.

The need or desire to work outside the home together with other economic and sociological factors were the conditions that led Bronfenbrenner (1975, 1979) as well as others (Dunst, 1985; Dunst & Trivette, in press-a, in press-b; Foster, Berger, & McLean, 1981; Hobbs et al., 1984; Stoneman, 1985; Zigler & Berman, 1983) to argue that successful early intervention programs are more likely to be those that employ an ecological perspective of families and that we intervene to produce broader-based social systems changes. A basic premise of social systems theories is that different social settings and their members are interdependent and that events and changes in one unit reverberate and produce changes in other social units. More specifically, there is "concern for the progressive accommodations between a growing human organism and its immediate environment, and *the way in which this relation is mediated by forces emanating from remote regions in the larger physical and social milieu* [italics added]" (Bronfenbrenner, 1979, p. 3). Consequently, the behavior of a child, his or her siblings, parents, and other family members may be affected by events in settings in which the child or parent may not even be present.

Both theoretical and empirical reasons exist to support the contention that needs (aspirations, goals, personal projects, etc.) are at least one major *set of forces* that affect the behavior of different family members and that needs often are generated by events and circumstances both within and outside the family unit (Dunst & Leet, 1987; Dunst & Trivette, in press-a; Fisher, Nadler, & DePaulo, 1983; Garbarino, 1982; Little, 1983; Palys, 1980). Moreover, there is evidence that lack of consensus between what professionals and families see as needs often sets the occasion for both conflict and a family's failure to follow professionally prescribed regimens. The latter is often interpreted by professionals as resistant, uncooperative, and noncompliant behavior (Merton, Merton, & Barber, 1983). However, what may be viewed as either oppositional or apathetic behavior may have less to do with contempt for professional opinion and more to do with lack of consensus regarding the nature of the presenting problem, the need for treatment (medical, educational, therapeutic, etc.), and the course of action that should be taken. As noted by Merton (1976), people that occupy different positions in a social structure (client vs. professional, low socioeconomic status vs. middle socioeconomic status, etc.) tend to differ in terms of what constitutes individual and family needs, and therefore how one should allocate time and energy to meet needs. In this book we discuss how needs affect behavior, how intrafamily and extrafamily resources can be used to meet needs, and how professionals can help families acquire the skills necessary to mobilize resources to meet needs. We both describe and elaborate upon a strategy recommended by Hobbs et al. (1984) in terms of the goal of family-level assessment and intervention from a social systems perspective. According to these investigators, "the goal [of family systems intervention] is to identify family needs, locate the informal and formal resources [and support] for meeting those needs, and help link families with the identified resources" (p. 50). To the extent that this can be done in a way that makes a family more competent and better able to mobilize intrafamily and extrafamily resources, which in turn promotes child, parent, and family functioning (Dunst, 1986a; Dunst & Trivette, 1987, in press-c), the family will have become empowered *par excellence*. Because the major focus of our assessment and intervention efforts is to enable and empower families in a way that makes them more competent and better able to mobilize resources, we will begin with a description of what we mean when we use the term "empowerment" in order to place the material described in this book in proper perspective.

A Social Systems Perspective of Empowerment

A number of definitions of empowerment can be found in the literature (Brickman et al., 1982; Dunst, 1985; Hobbs et al., 1984; Solomon, 1985). Three characteristics of these definitions have guided the ways in which we typically define and attempt to operationalize empowerment. These include a person's (1) access and control over needed resources, (2) decision-making and problem-solving abilities, and (3) acquisition of instrumental behavior needed to interact effectively with others to procure resources. Although this is a useful approach to defining empowerment, it has nonetheless constrained our understanding of what it means to be empowered and how we can go about enabling and empowering families. Indeed, we would go so far as to say that the problem-solving and decision-making approach to conceptualizing empowerment, which focuses almost entirely on the help seeker's behavior without consideration of the help giver's role in helping relationships, has restricted our understanding of empowerment because it fails to consider explicitly a number of broader-based issues as part of help-seeker and help-giver exchanges.[1]

A fuller understanding of empowerment requires that we take a broader-based view of the conditions that influence the behavior of people during help-seeker and help-giver exchanges. A social systems perspective seems to offer this type of framework and is perhaps best reflected in Rappaport's (1981) contention that:

> Empowerment implies that many competencies are already present or at least possible. . . . Empowerment implies that what you see as poor functioning is a result of social structure and lack of resources which make it impossible for the existing competencies to operate. It implies that in those cases where new competencies need to be learned, they are best learned in a context of living life rather than in artificial programs where everyone, including the person learning, knows that it is really the expert who is in charge. (p. 16)

This set of assertions includes three conditions that we believe reflect the way in which we need to think about helping relationships and empowerment. First, it states that people are already competent or that they have the capacity to become competent. This is what we refer to as a *proactive* stance as part of helping relationships. Second, it states that the failure to display competence is not due to deficits within the person but rather the failure of social systems to create opportunities for competencies to be displayed. Creating opportunities for competence to be displayed is what we refer to as *enabling* experiences. Third, it implicitly states that the person who is the help seeker, learner, or client must attribute behavior change to his or her own actions if one is to acquire a sense of control necessary to manage family affairs. This is what we mean when we say a person is *empowered*. Collectively, these three assertions provide a basis for viewing empowerment from a broader-based social systems perspective that suggests the importance of the help giver's behavior as part of both enabling and empowering families. As will be noted throughout this book, *it is not simply a matter of whether or not family needs are met, but rather the manner in which needs are met that is likely to be both enabling and empowering*. The methods described in this book are designed to help professionals engage in help-giving exchanges that increase the likelihood of a family becoming empowered as part of the family's efforts to meet its own needs.

Rethinking Family Intervention Practices

We want to note at the outset that we are asking the reader to "rethink" the ways in which he or she views families as well as the ways he or she engages in helping relationships. For some this rethinking will come easy; for others it will be a difficult process. Those who are in fundamental agreement with the major theses of our approach to working with families can become comfortable with the rethinking process we present and elaborate on. The ways in which we believe we need to rethink intervention practices with families include:

1. adoption of a social systems perspective of families that suggests a new and expanded definition of intervention (Dunst, 1985; Dunst & Trivette, in press-a)
2. movement beyond the child as the sole focus of intervention toward the family as the unit of intervention (Hobbs, 1975; Hobbs et al., 1984)
3. major emphasis upon empowerment of families as the goal of intervention practices (Rappaport, 1981, 1987)
4. a proactive stance toward families that places major emphasis upon promotion of growth-producing behavior rather than treatment of problems or prevention of negative outcomes (Dunst & Trivette, 1987)
5. focus on family and not professionally identified needs and aspirations as the primary targets of intervention (Dunst & Leet, 1987)
6. major emphasis on identifying and building upon family capabilities as a way of strengthening families (Hobbs et al., 1984)
7. major emphasis upon strengthening the family's personal social network and utilizing this network as a primary source of support and resources for meeting needs (Gottlieb, 1983)
8. a shift and expansion in the roles professionals play in interactions with families and the ways in which these roles are performed (Slater & Wikler, 1986; Solomon, 1985; Trivette, Deal, & Dunst, 1986)

Social Systems Perspective

A social systems perspective views a family as a social unit embedded within other formal and informal social units and networks. It also views these different social networks as interdependent where events and changes in one unit resonate and in turn directly and indirectly influence the behavior of individuals in other social units. A social systems perspective also considers events within and between social units as supportive and health-promoting to the extent that they have positive influences on family functioning. Collectively, these various relationships provide a basis for proposing a social systems definition of intervention as the *provision of support (i.e., resources provided by others) by members of a family's informal and formal social network that either directly or indirectly influences child, parent, and family functioning.* This type of social systems perspective of families and intervention is reflected in Bronfenbrenner's (1979) words on parenting tasks:

> Whether parents can perform effectively in their child-rearing roles within the family depends on the *role demands, stresses, and supports emanating from other settings* [italics added]. . . . Parents' evaluations of their own capacity to

function, as well as their view of their child, are related to such external factors as *flexibility of job schedules, adequacy of child care arrangements, the presence of friends and neighbors who can help out in large and small emergencies* [italics added], the quality of health and social services, and neighborhood safety. The availability of supportive settings is, in turn, a function of their existence and frequency in a given culture or subculture. This frequency can be enhanced by the adoption of public policies and practices that create additional settings and societal roles conducive to family life. (p. 7)

Unit of Intervention

Considering the family, and not the child, as the unit of intervention recognizes that the family system is comprised of interdependent members and that by strengthening and supporting the family unit and not just the child the chances of making a significant positive impact upon *ALL* family members are enhanced considerably. Enabling parents to meet the needs of all family members is valued because it promotes the acquisition of competencies that in turn make parents better able to have the time, energy, and resources necessary for enhancing the well-being and development of other family members. As noted by Hobbs et al. (1984):

> Families are the critical element in the rearing of healthy, competent, and caring children. We suggest, however that families—all *families—cannot perform this function as well as they might unless they are supported by a caring and strong community, for it is community (support) that provides the informal and formal supplements to families' own resources* [italics added]. Just as a child needs nurturance, stimulation, and the resources that caring adults bring to his or her life, so, too, do parents—as individuals and as adults filling socially valued roles (for example, parent, worker)—need the resources made possible by a caring community if they are to fulfill their roles well. (p. 46)

Empowerment of Families

The ability of families to manage life events effectively as well as gain mastery over their affairs requires that we empower families to become competent and capable rather than dependent upon professional helpers or helping systems. This is accomplished by creating opportunities for families to acquire the necessary knowledge and skills to become stronger and better able to manage and negotiate the many demands and forces that impinge upon the family unit in a way that promotes individual and family well-being. Deriving pleasure and gratification in seeing others become competent and capable is a fundamental attribute of a helping professional who is a proponent of an empowerment philosophy. To the extent that we do not recognize and explicitly consider empowerment of families as the goal of intervention, we are more likely to fool ourselves into believing that we have done a good job when in fact we have lost an opportunity to enable and empower the family and perhaps have even created dependencies by engaging in noncontingent helping.[2] As Rappaport (1981) has so aptly pointed out, most of what we do in the name of helping is usurping rather than empowering.

> The pervasive belief that experts should solve all of [the help seeker's] problems in living has created a social and cultural iatrogenesis which extends the sense of alienation and loss of ability to control [one's] life. . . . This is the path that the social as well as the physical health experts have been on, and we need to reverse this trend. (p. 17)

Proactive Positive Promotion

A proactive approach to helping relationships views families—*all* families—in a positive light and places major emphasis upon promoting the acquisition of self-sustaining and adaptive behaviors that emphasize growth among all family members and not just an individual child. Acceptance of individual differences is valued because "it encourages a more productive approach to intervention in which we do not try to change children [and their families] but instead try to build on the strengths that they bring to the [helping relationship]" (Zigler & Berman, 1983, p. 895). A proactive approach focuses on family strengths and capabilities in a way that supports and strengthens family functioning. To the extent possible, the focus of all intervention efforts is on promoting the acquisition of knowledge and skills that makes the family more competent, thus strengthening family functioning. In contrast to treatment strategies that *correct* problems or disorders and prevention strategies that *decrease the risk* of problems or disorders (both of which are deficit-oriented), a promotion approach to working with families emphasizes positive targets as the goal of intervention, not the alleviation or reduction of negative outcomes. The three Ps of this maxim—proactive, positive, and promotion—are perhaps best reflected in our paraphrasing of Carkhuff and Anthony's (1979) definition of helping restated in terms of a family focus:

> Helping is the act of *promoting* and *supporting* family functioning in a way that *enhances* the acquisition of competencies that permit a greater degree of *intrafamily* control over subsequent activities.

Family Needs and Aspirations

The focus on family and not professionally identified needs and aspirations as the target of intervention recognizes the family's rightful role in deciding what is most important and in the best interest of the family unit and its members. According to Hobbs (1975), "the foresighted professional person knows that it is the parent who truly bears the responsibility for the child, and the parent cannot be replaced by episodic professional service" (pp. 228–229). Responsive and truly individualized interventions address the needs and aspirations of the family by promoting the family's ability to identify and meet its needs in a way that makes the family more capable and competent. This approach to working with families was stated in the following way by Pilisuk and Parks (1986) in terms of the relationship between the help seeker's and help giver's roles as part of social support interventions:

> The [family] defines the need for service. A need for assistance is not assumed until the [family] has set forth such a need. This request for assistance might originate with one individual or with the . . . [family] system. . . . The social support facilitator helps the [family] crystallize the [concern]. (pp. 162–163)

Family Strengths

All families have strengths and capabilities. If we take the time to identify these qualities and build on them rather than focus on correcting deficits or weaknesses, families are not only more likely to respond favorably to interventions but the chances of making a significant positive impact on the family unit are enhanced considerably. A major consideration of strengthening families is promoting their ability to use existing strengths for meeting needs in a way that produces positive changes in family functioning. According to Garbarino (1982):

> The crucial property of families, and systems in general, is that the whole and its parts must be able to [achieve their aspirations] for both to continue. A family "works" when its members feel good about the family, *when their needs are being met* [italics added], and the development of relationships flow smoothly. (p. 72)

Informal Support and Resources

A family's personal social network generally has a wealth of support and resources that can be used to meet needs and attain aspirations, yet there is a tendency for professionals to supplant or replace natural support systems with professional services. To the extent possible and appropriate, major emphasis is placed upon strengthening and building natural support systems that create positive, proactive linkages among the members of the family's support network. The importance of doing so is reflected in Gottlieb's (1983) observations that

> When people recognize that they [have needs] they [generally] consult family members, friends, workmates, and neighbors, calling upon them for advice about *community resources that are best matched to their needs.* (p. 210)

Professional Roles

Meeting the individualized needs of families requires not only a shift and expansion in the roles professionals assume in interactions with families, but also a significant change in the ways in which these roles are performed. According to Rappaport (1981), the ability to empower and strengthen families in a way that makes them more competent and capable "requires a breakdown of the typical role relationship(s) between professionals and community people" (p. 19). Partnerships are valued over paternalistic approaches because the former implies and conveys the belief that partners are capable individuals who become more capable by sharing knowledge, skills, and resources in a manner that leaves all participants better off after entering into the cooperative arrangement. As noted by Dunst (1985):

> [Helping relationships] that utilize partnerships avoid viewing (individual and family) differences as deficits that have some pathological origins that must be "treated" as an illness. Rather, differences arising from intra- and extra-family influences are seen as conditions that *generate needs that can best be met by mobilizing resources that allow these needs to be met and thus strengthen families* [italics added]. (p. 171)

These considerations collectively form the basis of the assessment and intervention model described in this book. These distinct but interrelated maxims serve as guidelines and principles for the conduct of a family systems approach to empowering families to be able to meet their needs in a way that is growth-producing. The conceptual and philosophical underpinnings of our model are reflected in the social systems, family-as-unit-of-intervention, empowerment, and proactive orientation that we have adopted in our work with families. The operational and application-in-practice aspects of the model are reflected in the needs and aspirations, family strengths, support and resources, and professional roles (help-giving behavior) features of the model.

At this point we will briefly describe the last four maxims to help the reader understand the particular point of view that we propose as part of engaging in family-level, needs-based assessment and intervention practices.

Overview of the
Assessment and Intervention Model

Figure 1-1 shows the four operational components of the model and relationships among the components. Family needs and aspirations, family strengths and capabilities (family functioning style), and social support and resources are viewed as separate but interdependent parts of the assessment and intervention process. The help-giving behaviors used by professionals are the ways in which families are enabled and empowered to acquire and use competencies to procure support and mobilize resources for meeting needs. Needs and resources, family strengths and capabilities, and support and resources may be thought of as sets of interlocking gears, whereas help-giving behavior may be thought of the mechanism for aligning the gears in a way that makes the parts of the system optimally efficient.

The operationalization of the process may be described as follows: Family needs and aspirations are first identified to determine what a family considers important enough to devote its time and energy. Second, the unique ways in which the family system operates are identified to determine how the family typically

Figure 1-1.

Four Major Components
of the Assessment and Intervention Model
and Their Relationships.

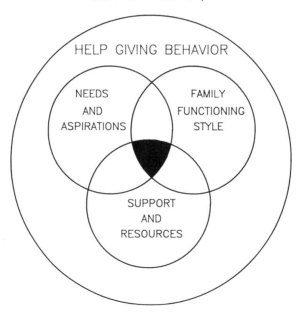

deals with life's trials and tribulations and what aspects of the family system are working well. Third, the family's personal social network is "mapped" to identify existing and potential sources of aid and assistance that may be procured and mobilized to meet needs and achieve aspirations. Fourth, the optimal alignment and integration of the three parts of the family system occur, in part, by the help-giving behaviors (professional roles) that are employed as part of the assessment and intervention process.

Our assessment and intervention model is best described as a *dynamic, fluid process* that is continually operationalized each and every time the help giver interacts with a family. The ability to carry out our assessment and intervention model is a *craft* that can be learned if one is willing to devote the time and energy to master the necessary material and to practice and perfect the skills needed to work effectively with families. Learning, practicing, and perfecting the craft should provide the help giver with a set of skills and competencies that permits him or her to promote a family's ability to mobilize support and resources to meet needs and attain aspirations in a way that is both enabling and empowering.

Notes

1. The terms "help seeker" and "help giver," borrowed from the helping relationships literature (DePaulo, Nadler, & Fisher, 1983; Fisher, Nadler, & DePaulo, 1983; Nadler, Fisher, & DePaulo, 1983), are used throughout the book to refer to what is typically described as the client and professional, respectively. However, because help givers include members of a family's personal social network (spouse, mate, kin, friend, etc.) as well as other informal sources of support (e.g., the church), we employ the more inclusive helping relationships terms in this book.

2. Noncontingent helping or giving is potentially one of the most damaging aspects of help-giver behavior. It refers to situations where the help seeker plays little or no active role in procuring resources necessary to meet needs as a result of the help giver directly or indirectly interfering with the family's ability to become more capable and competent. According to Skinner (1978), "We may not really help others by doing things for them. . . . By giving much help we postpone the acquisition of effective behavior and perpetuate the need for help" (pp. 250–251). By giving too much, we usurp family opportunities to become capable, and by perpetuating the need for help, we foster help-seeker dependencies on the help giver.

2

Needs, Aspirations, and Family Functioning

The operationalization of the needs-based approach to assessment and intervention proposed by Hobbs et al. (1984) requires that we have a working knowledge of the meaning of need and the ways in which needs influence behavior.

Needs, Environmental Press, and Needs Hierarchies

Definition of Need

A need is something (e.g., a resource) that is desired or lacking but wanted or required to achieve a goal or attain a particular end. Operationally, a need is an individual's judgment of the discrepancy between actual states or conditions and what is considered normative, desired, or valued *from a help seeker's and not a help giver's perspective*. Unless there is an indicated need for a resource on the part of a help seeker, there may not be a need regardless of what a professional believes to be the case.

There are several distinct characteristics of need identification implicit in the above definition (McKillip, 1987; Reid, 1985).

1. There must be some concern, problem, or perception that something is not as it ought to be. This is referred to as *psychological awareness*. An awareness of the difference (discrepancy) between what is and what ought to be must be present if a person is to consider his or her condition different enough to warrant action to alleviate or reduce the discrepancy.

2. The role that personal values and phenomenological beliefs play in determining a need must not only be taken into consideration but must be explicitly recognized as one set of conditions that defines concerns or problems. This is referred to as *value influence*. On the one hand, the mere recognition of a discrepancy between what is and what ought to be is not sufficient to define a condition as problematic unless the person makes a personal judgment that the discrepancy is currently or will potentially influence his or her behavior. On the other hand, we must take a person's assessment of his or her situation seriously as part of need identification. As Thomas and Thomas (1928) noted 50 years ago, "if [people] define situations as real, they are real in their consequences" (p. 572).

3. There must be some evaluation or awareness that there is a resource that will reduce the discrepancy between what is and what ought to be. The desire for the resource is referred to as *need recognition*. Need recognition occurs whenever something (e.g., a resource) is identified as a form of aid or assistance that will reduce the perceived discrepancy.

4. There must be a recognition that there is a way of procuring a resource to meet the need before a discrepancy is perceived as amendable to help. This is referred to as *solution identification*. In many cases people do not perceive themselves as having needs if they see no way in which resources can be procured to meet them regardless of the existence of the resources.

That these different conditions contribute to need identification can be illustrated with an experience recently shared with us by one of our staff. This individual was making a home visit to a family referred to our program. It happened that it was raining when the staff member arrived at the family's home. Upon entering the house, this individual could not but notice that there was a gaping hole in the roof with water pouring into the living room. She also could not help but notice that the situation did not seem to bother the family in the least. The staff member didn't comment on what she observed and went about her business of explaining our program and describing the ways in which we work with families. During the course of the conversation and after establishing rapport with the family, the staff member casually asked how the hole had gotten in the roof. The family told her what happened and went on to explain that they rented the house, couldn't get the landlord to fix the hole, couldn't get the landlord to pay for the materials and let the family fix the roof, and didn't have enough money to buy the materials to make the repairs. The family also indicated that they learned to "live with the inconvenience" because they saw no way of getting the resources necessary to correct the situation. The family did not see their condition as a need because they exhausted all solutions to the problem.[1]

As this example illustrates, different characteristics of the above needs identification process must be present before a condition or concern is defined as a need. As will be seen, the ability to recognize and bear in mind the potential influence of all four characteristics described above is an important part of needs identification.

Use of Terminology

Our definition of need makes any number of terms appropriate for describing the discrepancy between actual and desired states. Several of these are shown in Figure 2-1 as a subset of the more inclusive term "need." When we use the term "need," we mean any perception of importance or urgency that results in a family allocating time, energy, or resources to reduce the discrepancy between *what is* and *what is desired*. The various terms shown in Figure 2-1 will be used interchangeably throughout this book, although the terms "needs," "aspirations," and "projects" are used primarily since they are most consistent with the assessment and intervention process we describe.

Needs Categories

According to Hartman and Laird (1983), "the term 'need' undoubtedly should be viewed in relative terms" (p. 164). Nonetheless, it is possible to specify major categories of needs as well as order needs along a continuum from the most to the least basic (Dunst & Leet, 1987; Hartman & Laird, 1983; Trivette et al., 1986). The major categories of needs include at least the following: financial adequacy; food and shelter; health and protection; communication and mobility; vocational opportunities; availability of time; education, enrichment, and growth; emotional stability; and cultural/social involvement (see Table 2–1 on pp. 18 & 19). As we shall see, this broader-based conceptualization of needs not only expands what constitutes appropriate targets of intervention, but expands the roles professionals play in helping families meet their needs.

Environmental Press and Personal Projects

An understanding of environmental press helps explain the manner in which needs influence behavior. Garbarino (1982) defined environmental press as:

... the combined influence of forces working in an environment to shape the behavior and development of individuals in that setting. It arises from the circumstances confronting and surrounding an individual that generate [needs and] psychosocial momentum, which *tend to guide that individual in a particular direction* [italics added]. (p. 13)

This suggests that forces that are strongest will take precedence and steer behavior in certain directions. Thus, a person's perception of what constitutes the most important needs at a particular time will likely assume priority status, guide the person's behavior, and consume his or her time and energy.

The notion of personal projects is a concept closely related to environmental press and helps expand our understanding of how different events shape and influence a person's behavior. Little (1983) defined personal projects as a "set of interrelated acts extending over time, which is intended to maintain or attain a state of affairs foreseen by the individual" (p. 276). Personal projects include any activity, event, or goal that is *viewed as important enough for an individual to devote his or her time and energy.* Personal projects include such things as securing employment; graduating from school; gaining parenting experience; aspi-

Figure 2-1.

The Relationship Among Terms
Used Interchangeably for "Need."

rations for self, child or family; or any other outcome that is personally important to a person and thus constitutes a need or aspiration. We find the idea of projects particularly appealing because it moves the focus of family-level assessment and intervention beyond rectification of problems toward a growth-producing emphasis. Although we use the term "need" throughout the book to refer to family-prioritized goals, we suggest that the term "family projects" may eventually be a more useful one for structuring family-level assessment and intervention practices.[2]

Needs and Need Hierarchies

The proposition that individual and family needs are forces that affect behavior is fundamental to family systems theory (Hartman & Laird, 1983). Moreover, because needs can be roughly ordered in a hierarchy from the most to least important, emphasis is likely to be placed on meeting unmet needs that are at the top of the hierarchy (i.e., those that are personally most important). The contention that needs can be ordered on a continuum and both steer and propel behavior is not new. These notions can be traced to Lewin's (1931) field theory of environmental psychology, Hull's (1943) and Murray's (1938) theories of motivation, and Maslow's (1954) theory of self-actualization. Maslow, for example, placed needs in a hierarchy, and argued that unmet basic needs dominate behavior and interfere with achievement of higher-level needs. In our work with families, we find that needs and needs hierarchies are highly personalized and unique to individual families. This necessitates not only an individualized approach to identifying needs but also ordering them in a priority sequence from the family's and not the help giver's perspective.

When embedded within a social systems framework, needs and need hierarchies take on new meaning, especially in terms of assessment and intervention practices. In our work with families of preschool age children, we have repeatedly come to the realization that lack of family resources negatively affects health and well-being and decreases the probability that professionally prescribed, child-level interventions will be carried out by the child's care givers when the prescription is not identified as a high-priority family need. When needs go unmet, this condition acts as a force that presses the family to invest emotional and physical time and energy to meet these needs. This in turn takes its toll on personal well-being and health, makes attention to professionally prescribed regimens a low priority, and is most likely to occur when professional recommendations do not involve actions designed to meet family-identified needs. Thus, a family who fails to adhere to a professionally prescribed regimen may do so not because its members are resistant, uncooperative, or noncompliant, but because the family's circumstances steer behavior in other directions.

Table 2-1.

A Taxonomy of Need Categories for Structuring Efforts To Identify Needs.

Need Categories/Needs	Need Categories/Needs
Economic	**Adult Education/Enrichment**
Money for necessities	Availability of appropriate adult educational opportunities
Budgeting financial resources	Accessibility of educational opportunities
Money for special needs/projects	Opportunities to play/interact with own children
Money for the future	
Stable income	**Child Education/Intervention**
	Child education opportunities
Physical	Access/availability of specialized intervention services
Clean environment	Opportunities to interact/play with other children
Adequate housing (space, safety, furnishings)	Access to integrated community experiences
Safe neighborhood (protection)	
Adequate heat and water	**Child Care**
Accessibility of other physical resources	Help in routine child care
	Emergency child care

Food/Clothing
Adequate and balanced diet
Enough clean clothes for each season

Medical/Dental
Confidence in medical/dental professionals
Availability of routine/emergency health care
Accessibility of medical/dental care

Vocational
Opportunity to work
Satisfaction with work (in or outside the home)
Job security

Transportation/Communication
Means for transporting family members to and from
    needed resources
Means for contacting relatives, friends, etc.
Access to a telephone

Availability of day care/baby sitting

Recreational
Opportunities for recreational activities for individual
    family members and the family unit
Availability of recreational activities for individual
    family members, couple, total family

Emotional
Positive intrafamily relationships
Positive relationships outside the family
Companionship
Sense of belonging to family or other group
Opportunities to spend time with significant others

Cultural/Social
Opportunities to share ethnic or value-related
    experiences with others
Opportunities to be involved with community/cultural affairs
Accessibility of community/cultural affairs

Need Hierarchies
and Family Functioning

The extent to which unmet needs affect well-being and interfere with implementation of professionally prescribed regimens has been tested in three studies conducted in our program (Dunst & Leet, 1987; Dunst, Vance, & Cooper, 1986; Trivette & Dunst, in preparation). The subjects were parents of handicapped, retarded, and developmentally at-risk children in two of the studies and teen-age mothers in the other investigation. In each study, the parents completed either the Family Resource Scale (Dunst & Leet, 1987) or the Support Functions Scale (Dunst & Trivette, 1985a), both of which assess needs and adequacy of resources. In each of the studies, the parents also completed well-being measures that assessed both their physical and emotional health. In two of the studies, the parents were asked to indicate the extent to which they had the time, energy, and personal investment (commitment) to carry out child-level educational and therapeutic interventions (Dunst & Leet, 1987; Dunst, Vance, & Cooper, 1986).

The results from all three studies supported our expectations. Dunst and Leet (1987) found a correlation of .56 ($p<.001$), Dunst, Vance, and Cooper (1986) a correlation of .45 ($p<.05$), and Trivette and Dunst (in preparation) a correlation of .34 ($p<.001$) between parent assessment of needs and personal well-being. The greater the number of unmet needs, the greater the number of emotional and physical problems reported by the parents. With respect to commitment to carrying out child-level interventions, Dunst and Leet (1987) found a correlation of .53 ($p<.001$) and Dunst, Vance, and Cooper (1986) a correlation of .54 ($p<.01$) between need scores and the commitment measures. The greater the number of needs unrelated to child-level interventions, the greater the probability that the parents indicated they did not have the time, energy, and personal investment to carry out such interventions. The relationships between needs and both well-being and commitment were still significant even when the effects of parents' age and education, family SES and income, and child age and Developmental Quotient (DQ) were first statistically partialled from the correlations between adequacy of resources and both well-being and adherence to prescribed regimens.

Implications

A needs hierarchy perspective of environmental press has at least two major implications for working with families. First, the relationships between family resources, well-being, and adherence to prescribed regimens indicates that before parents are asked to carry out professionally prescribed, child-level interventions, efforts to meet other family-identified needs must be made for parents to have the time and energy to work with their own children in an educational or therapeutic capacity. Second, if parents are asked to function in an educational or therapeutic capacity where the family indicates they have other, more pressing needs, the added demands placed upon the family system is likely to result in any number of negative consequences, including added stress, negative feelings toward the child, and alienation between the parents and help giver. Available data clearly indicate a need to move beyond educational targets as the sole focus of intervention toward a broader-based social systems perspective as part of early intervention practices if we are to be truly responsive to the changing and evolving needs of families.

Notes

1. As it so happened, the major thrust of one of the services that the staff member was explaining to the family was to enable families to meet their needs through the exchange of resources among the members of an informal share network. The very next day, the family "bartered" a resource needed by a member of the share network in exchange for this person fixing the roof for the family.

2. We also find the term "project" more appealing because it implies something valued or important and, unlike the term "need," does not put goals or aspirations on a continuum that is often interpreted on a bad-to-good or weakness-to-strength dimension—despite the fact that the term "need," by definition, is not a notion that implies such an either/or valuation.

3

Resources, Social Support, and Family Functioning

In our work to identify the best ways to help families acquire the skills necessary to secure aid and assistance to meet needs, we have found it useful to differentiate between intrafamily and extrafamily resources. Pearlin and Schooler (1978) make a distinction between social and psychological resources that helps define the parameters of these two different sets of resources. Social resources are the sources of support and external resources potentially available to a family that may be accessed in times of need. Psychological resources include the inter- and intra-individual family member characteristics that are used to respond to *crisis* situations, *cope* with normative and nonnormative life events, and *promote* growth and development in all family members. We refer to the last type of resource as *family functioning style* and the first type of resource as *social support*.

Family Resources and Family Functioning Style

The ways in which families cope with life events as well as promote the growth and development of family members is partly dependent upon a family's unique functioning style. Family functioning style refers to a combination of both existing strengths and capabilities and the capacity to use these strengths to mobilize or create resources necessary to meet needs.

Although family strengths are generally recognized as one set of resources for meeting needs, it is surprising how little we know about family strengths. As Otto (1963) pointed out 25 years ago:

> Although the professional literature is replete with criteria for identifying "problem families" and criteria useful in the diagnosis of family problems or family disorganization, little is known about how we might identify a "strong family." (p. 329)

It is remarkable how few advances have been made since Otto first made this claim. This state of affairs makes the process of identifying intrafamily resources difficult at best. What we do know about strong families comes from a suggestive but incomplete family strengths literature.

Definition of Family Strengths

According to Williams, Lindgren, Rowe, VanZandt, & Stinnet (1985):

> Family strengths refers to those relationship patterns, *interpersonal skills and competencies, and social and psychological characteristics* [italics added] which create a sense of positive family identity, promote satisfying and fulfilling interaction among family members, encourage the development of the potential of the family group and individual family members, and contribute to the family's ability to deal effectively with stress and crisis. (Preface)

Similarly, Otto (1975) defined family strengths as:

> . . . those *forces and dynamic factors* [italics added] . . . which encourage the development of the personal resources and potentials of members of the family and which make family life deeply satisfying and fulfilling to family members. (p. 16)

On the one hand, these definitions indicate that family strengths are primarily interpersonal and intrafamily in nature. On the other hand, they suggest that strengths are influenced by forces both within and outside the family unit. Both features of these definitions of family strengths are consistent with the social systems framework described above.

Qualities of Strong Families

The pioneering work of Otto (1962, 1963) forms the basis of current family strengths research. The most ambitious work to date on family strengths has been conducted by Stinnett and his collegues (Stevenson, Lee, Stinnett, & DeFrain, 1983; Stinnett, 1979, 1980, 1985; Stinnett & DeFrain, 1985a; Stinnett, Knorr, DeFrain, & Rowe, 1981; Stinnett, Lynn, Kimmons, Fuenning, & DeFrain, 1984) who have obtained extensive information from families about the characteristics that define strong families. Curran's (1983) work, on the other hand, has attempted to identify the traits of healthy (strong) families from the perspective of professionals with extensive but varied experiences working with families. There is remarkable congruence between the findings of Stinnett et al. and Curran on the characteristics that contribute to a positive family functioning style.

The work of Stinnett et al. and Curran as well as others (Hill, 1971; Lewis, Beavers, Gossett, & Phillips, 1976; Otto, 1975; Satir, 1972) suggests that there are about 12 major, nonmutually exclusive qualities of strong families. Before listing these characteristics, however, it should be made explicitly clear that not all strong families are characterized by the presence of all 12 qualities. *A combination of qualities appears to define strong families, with certain combinations defining unique family functioning styles.* As Lewis et al. (1976) demonstrated, "optimally functioning or competent families appears to be [due to] the presence and interrelationship of a number of variables" (p. 205). With this caveat, the 12 qualities include:

1. a belief and sense of *commitment* toward promoting the well-being and growth of individual family members as well as that of the family unit
2. *appreciation* for the small and large things that individual family members do well and encouragement to do better
3. concentrated effort to spend *time* and do things together, no matter how formal or informal the activity or event
4. a sense of *purpose* that permeates the reasons and basis for "going on" in both bad and good times
5. a sense of *congruence* among family members regarding the value and importance of assigning time and energy to meet needs
6. the ability to *communicate* with one another in a way that emphasizes positive interactions
7. a clear set of family *rules*, *values*, and *beliefs* that establishes expectations about acceptable and desired behavior
8. a varied repertoire of *coping strategies* that promote positive functioning in dealing with both normative and nonnormative life events
9. the ability to engage in *problem-solving* activities designed to evaluate options for meeting needs and procuring resources

10. the ability to be *positive* and see the positive in almost all aspects of their lives, including the ability to see crisis and problems as an opportunity to learn and grow
11. *flexibility* and *adaptability* in the roles necessary to procure resources to meet needs
12. a *balance* between the use of internal and external family resources for coping and adapting to life events and planning for the future

Two major themes emerge from examination of the literature upon which these 12 qualities are based. The first is that family strengths and capabilities represent intrafamily resources that are often mobilized as one way to meet needs. The second is that family strengths and capabilities are the competencies that families employ to mobilize or create extrafamily resources. The presence of different qualities, as well as their unique combinations, defines what we have come to call *family functioning style*.

Family Functioning Style

The ability to take family strengths into consideration as part of intervention practices is important in work with families. However, we believe there is danger in using the word "strength" to refer to family capabilities because the term implies a continuum, with strengths at one end and weaknesses at the opposite end. We prefer the term "family functioning style" because it implies *unique* ways of dealing with life events and promoting growth and development. There are no right or wrong family functioning styles, but rather differentially effective styles that are likely to be employed in response to different life events and situations. The work of Pearlin and Schooler (1978) and Folkman and her colleagues (1980, 1984, 1985, 1986) on the structure and utilization of coping mechanisms supports this contention. These investigators found that people employ different coping behaviors in response to different life events and that the resources that a person has available define coping style. We suggest that families also have various types of strengths and competencies that collectively define their unique family functioning style and that these styles reflect the ways in which families cope and grow. Indeed, the presence and combination of different psychological characteristics constitute the defining features of unique functioning styles (Lewis et al., 1976; Pearlin & Schooler, 1978).

The importance of family strengths is partly dependent upon whether or not the various traits, qualities, and characteristics that define family functioning style are related to desired outcomes. There is a small but corroborative set of data that show positive relationships between different intrafamily characteristics and various behavior outcomes, including life satisfaction (Sanders, Walters, & Montgomery,

1985), emotional well-being and family cohesiveness (Stinnett et al., 1985), satisfaction with efforts to manage stressful occurrences (Folkman et al., 1986), and physical health (Lewis et al., 1976). Intrafamily resources, or family functioning styles, are one set of factors that have been found to be important for promoting health and well-being.

Implications

There are a number of major implications to be drawn from what we know about family strengths and family functioning style. First, the mere recognition of the existence of the qualities of strong families calls attention to the fact that *all* families have strengths that constitute valuable resources. Second, by both recognizing their presence and employing family strengths as one way of meeting needs, we build upon the very things that makes a particular family work well. Third, by building upon and strengthening the family's reservoir of resources, we make the family unit even stronger and more capable of negotiating the developmental course of both individual family members and the family unit. Help givers who work with families oftentimes overlook (and sometimes ignore) the fact that families have strengths that are intrafamily resources for meeting needs. We as help givers can be of most benefit to families by promoting their ability to identify and utilize their own family resources.

Social Support, Extrafamily Resources, and Family Functioning

In addition to being influenced by intrafamily resources and family functioning style, the ways in which families cope with life events as well as promote the growth and development of family members is in part dependent upon the sources of extrafamily support and resources available to the family unit and its members.

Definition of Social Support and Extrafamily Resources

It is well documented that extrafamily social support and resources are a major source of aid and assistance necessary for meeting individual and family needs (Cohen & Syme, 1985a; Fisher, Nadler, & Whitcher-Alagna, 1983). Social support is defined as "the resources provided by other persons . . . [and] differs in type and function . . . at different periods of life" (Cohen & Syme, 1985b, p. 4). A resource is defined as "something that lies ready for use or that can be drawn upon for aid or to take care of . . . in time of a need or emergency" (Webster's New World Dictionary, 1974, p. 1211). Extrafamily resources and social support include the emotional, physical, informational, instrumental, and material aid and assistance provided by others to maintain health and well-being, promote adaptations of life events, and foster development in an adaptative manner.

The sources of support and extrafamily resources potentially available to a family include relatives, friends, neighbors, co-workers, church associates, clubs and social organizations, day-care centers, and any other individual, group, or social organization that the family has contact with either directly or indirectly. Operationally, one can differentiate between *informal* and *formal* sources of social support. Informal support networks include both individuals (kin, friends, neighbors, minister, etc.) and social groups (church, social clubs, etc.) who are accessible to provide support as part of daily living, usually in response to both normative and nonnormative life events. Formal support networks include both professionals (physicians, infant specialists, social workers, therapists, etc.) and agencies (hospitals, early intervention programs, health departments, etc.) that are, on an *a priori* basis, formally organized to provide aid and assistance to persons seeking needed resources.

The Social Support Domain

A number of conceptual frameworks have been proposed for specifying the components of support as well as the relationships among those components (Barrera, 1986; Dunst & Trivette, in press-d; Hall & Wellman, 1985; House & Kahn, 1985; Kahn, Wethington & Ingersoll-Dayton, 1987; Tardy, 1985; Turner, 1983). An integration of evidence regarding the social support domain suggests that it is comprised of five major components: relational, structural, constitutional, and functional support and support satisfaction.

Relational support refers to the existence and quantity of social relationships, including such things as marital and work status, number of persons in one's social network, and membership in social organizations such as the church. The existence of social relationships as well as the breadth of these relationships are important because they set the occasion for supportive exchanges.

Structural support refers to any number of quantitative aspects of social networks, including network density, stability and durability of relationships, intensity of feelings toward network members, and reciprocity of relationships (Hall & Wellman, 1985). The various features of structural support are designed as ways of capturing the nature of social relationships between people that are thought to be crucial for interactive exchanges to be supportive in nature (Gottlieb, 1981).

Figure 3-1. Five Major Components of the Social Support Domain and Their Relationships.

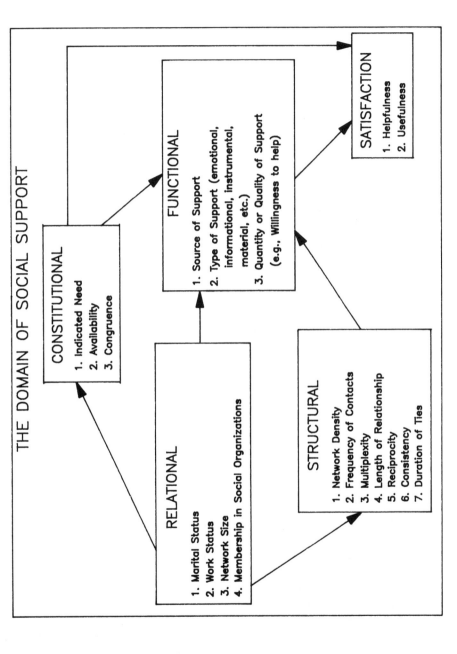

THE DOMAIN OF SOCIAL SUPPORT

CONSTITUTIONAL

1. Indicated Need
2. Availability
3. Congruence

FUNCTIONAL

1. Source of Support
2. Type of Support (emotional, informational, instrumental, material, etc.)
3. Quantity or Quality of Support (e.g., Willingness to help)

SATISFACTION

1. Helpfulness
2. Usefulness

RELATIONAL

1. Marital Status
2. Work Status
3. Network Size
4. Membership in Social Organizations

STRUCTURAL

1. Network Density
2. Frequency of Contacts
3. Multiplexity
4. Length of Relationship
5. Reciprocity
6. Consistency
7. Duration of Ties

Constitutional support refers to the indicated need for help, the availability of specific types of support that are needed, and the congruence (match) between needed support and the type of support offered. The notion of constitutional support has evolved from our own work on specifying the nature of supportive exchange and has emerged as one of the most important determinants of positive influences on family functioning (Trivette & Dunst, in preparation).

Functional support refers to the source, type, and both quantity and quality of help and assistance. This includes such things as informational, material, emotional, and instrumental aid and assistance and the *manner* in which it is procured or offered from different network members.

Support satisfaction refers to the extent to which assistance and aid are viewed as helpful and useful. During and at the completion of a social exchange, people generally evaluate subjectively the nature of the support provided by others.

As one might suspect, the five support components are conceptually, logically, and empirically related. Figure 3-1 (preceding page) shows the ways in which we believe the five components of support are related. The existence or quantity of relational support is viewed as a necessary condition for and hence a partial determinant of (1) defining needs (constitutional support), (2) the structural characteristics of one's social network, and (3) the types of help and assistance available from network members. Similarly, both constitutional needs and network structure may partially determine the particular types of support that are sought and offered. Finally, the types of support provided, especially the relationship between constitutional and functional support, will in part determine the degree to which one finds the aid and assistance helpful and thus the extent to which one is satisfied with the support. Taken together, these five components and the potential connections among them provide a basis for understanding the temporal and mediational relationships that set the occasion for supportive exchanges. Dunst and Trivette (in press-d) present evidence regarding the existence of ties between the five components of support and the extent to which these components are related to family functioning.

Support, Resources, and Family Functioning

Figure 3-2 shows a simplified version of how we believe social support affects parent, family, and child functioning. According to this model, social support influences parent well-being and health; support and well-being influence family functioning; support, well-being, and family functioning influence styles of parent-child interactions; and support, well-being, family functioning, and interactive styles influence child behavior and development. Within this framework of direct and indirect relationships, well-being, family functioning, and interactive styles

Figure 3-2.

A Model of the Direct and Indirect Influences
of Social Support.

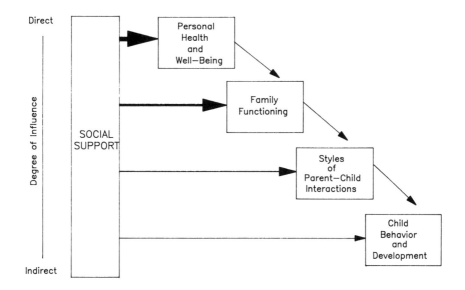

function as both independent and dependent variables depending upon the juncture at which one is assessing the influences of social support.

There is now a considerable amount of evidence that indicates that social support and extrafamily resources directly and indirectly influences parent, family, and child functioning, including *personal health and well-being* (Cohen & Syme, 1985a), *familial well-being* (Patterson & McCubbin, 1983), *adaptations to life crises* (Moos, 1986), *satisfaction with parenting* (Crnic, Greenberg, Ragozin, Robinson, & Basham, 1983), *attitudes toward one's child* (Colletta, 1981), *parental styles of interaction* (Trivette & Dunst, 1987a), *aspirations for self and child* (Lazar & Darlington, 1982), *child temperament* (Affleck, Tennen, Allen, & Gershman, 1986), and *child behavior and development*, (Crnic, Greenberg, & Slough, 1986). The majority of evidence from our own research establishing the relationship among resources; support; and parent, family, and child functioning is summarized in Dunst and Trivette (in press-a, in press-b). The results from our work have shown that adequacy of different types and forms of support, *especially aid and resources that match family identified needs*, promotes parent and family well-being, decreases time demands placed upon a family by a disabled or at-risk child, promotes positive care-giver interactive styles and decreases the display of interfering interactive styles, enhances positive parental perception of child functioning, and influences a number of child behavior characteristics (affect, temperament, and motivation).

There is one major and consistent finding from available social support research, regardless of the population that is studied. Informal support from personal network members has powerful stress-buffering and health-promoting influences. The effects of informal support are generally greater than that attributable to formal support sources. In our own research, the effects of informal support are so great that these influences cannot be ignored as a major form of intervention.[1] Indeed, we would go so far as to say that, to the extent possible, family needs should be met by promoting the use of informal rather than formal support sources.

The basis for this contention comes from several attempts to validate the broader-based, social systems definition of intervention proposed in Chapter 1. As stated earlier, intervention is the provision of support (i.e., resources provided by others) by members of a family's informal and formal social network that either directly or indirectly influences child, parent, and family functioning. This definition contrasts sharply with a traditional perspective, in which the term "intervention" is generally defined either at the level of program involvement (i.e., involved vs. not involved) or in terms of the provision of a specific professional therapeutic or educational treatment. We believe that this perspective of intervention is overly constricted because it both fails to recognize the potential effects of informal forms of support and has limited our understanding of how to empower and strengthen families effectively.

Evidence for a Broader-Based Definition of Intervention

The difference between a traditional and a social systems definition of intervention can be conceptually illustrated in terms of a percentage of variance interpretation of the effects of the treatment (intervention) variable.[2] The implicit assumption of a traditional perspective of intervention is that the major percentage of the variance accounted for in the outcome (dependent) variable is attributable to the intervention program or its program components and that the remaining percentage of variance not accounted for in the dependent variable is substantially error variance. In contrast, a social systems perspective of intervention assumes that beyond the percentage of variance accounted for by formal support, significant percentages of variance are attributable to other sources of support.

Dunst (1985) tested the validity of these contrasting views of intervention by assessing the degree to which parent, family, and child functioning was related to six sources of support: intrafamily (e.g., spouse or partner), formal kinship (e.g., own relatives, spouse's or partner's relatives), informal support (e.g., own friends, spouse's or partner's friends), social groups (e.g., social clubs, parent groups), early intervention (e.g., therapists, early intervention program staff), and other professionals (e.g., agencies, family physician). Of the ten dependent measures that were employed in this study, early intervention accounted for a significant percentage of variance in only one outcome variable (family opportunities [Holroyd, 1985]). In contrast, informal support accounted for a significant percentage of variance in nine of the ten outcome measures (e.g., parent well-being, time demands placed upon the family by the child, family integration, child behavior difficulties, and social acceptance [Holroyd, 1985]; parent expectations for the future of the child [Dunst & Trivette, 1986]; and number and frequency of parent-child play opportunities [Dunst, 1986b]). Intrafamily support accounted for a significant percentage of variance in five dependent measures (well-being, time demands, family integration, parent perceptions of child physical abilities, and number of parent-child play opportunities).

The findings from the Dunst (1985) study were subsequently replicated in a larger study involving 224 parents of retarded, handicapped, and developmentally at-risk preschoolers. The subjects were administered the Family Support Scale (Dunst, Jenkins, & Trivette, 1984) and completed the Parent-Child Play Scale (Dunst, 1986b) and selected subscales on the Questionnaire on Resources and Stress (Holroyd, 1985). The items on the Family Support Scale were grouped into four support categories: kinship support (spouse or partner, relatives, etc.), informal support (own friends, spouse's or partner's friends, other parents, church members), social groups (clubs, parent groups, etc.), and early intervention (therapists, teachers, school/day-care center staff, early intervention program staff). The subscale scores for each category were then correlated with each of the dependent measures. Kinship support accounted for a significant percentage of variance in three outcome measures (parent well-being, time demands placed upon the parents by their handicapped child, and family integration). Informal support accounted for a significant percentage of variance in four outcome measures (well-being, time demands, and both number and frequency of parent-child opportunities). Social group support accounted for a significant percentage of variance in frequency of parent-child play. The early intervention category was not related to any of the outcome measures.

Taken together, the findings from both the Dunst (1985) investigation and the replication study question the assumptions implicit in a traditional perspective of intervention (Dunst, 1986a; Dunst & Trivette, 1987) and provide support for the broad-based social system definition of intervention that we have adopted in working with families.

Implications

The availability of different types of informal and formal support as well as the relationships between social support and parent, family, and child functioning have a number of implications for intervention practices. First, the effects of informal social support on behavior and development indicate a need for an expanded definition of intervention (see Chapter 1). Intervention must be conceptualized as the aggregation of the many different types of help and assistance provided by members of a family's informal and formal support network. Second, the influences and contributions of support from a family's personal social network must be recognized and fully taken advantage of in terms of identifying resources for meeting needs. We as help givers cannot overlook or fail to recognize relatives, friends, neighbors, clergies, social clubs, and so forth as potential sources of support. Third, we must strive to match resources to needs with particular attention to the increased use of informal sources of support. By supporting and strengthening a family's personal social network, the probability of building long-lasting supportive linkages will be increased significantly.

Notes

1. There is one qualifier to this contention that must be mentioned. In our research with families of handicapped and at-risk children, we find that with certain parents our staff are not identified by the families as professionals but rather as members of their informal support network. The staff members who are considered personal network members are generally the ones who have created the types of partnership arrangements that we consider one of the conditions necessary for enabling and empowering families.

2. This conceptual and methodological approach may be represented by a number of circles of unit area. The procedure begins by defining all the variability in the outcome or dependent variable as well as the treatment or independent variables as equal to 100. The relationship between the outcome measure and a treatment variable is represented by the degree of overlap between the two circles. The amount of overlap defines what percentage of variance is accounted for in the dependent measure by the treatment variable.

4

Help-Giver Behavior
and Family Functioning

A fundamentally important aspect of help-seeker and help-giver exchanges, but one often neglected and overlooked as part of intervention practices, is the manner in which aid and assistance is offered and provided by informal and formal support network members. Both the help-seeking literature in general (Fisher, Nadler, & DePaulo, 1983) and that pertaining to handicapped children and their families specifically (Dunst & Trivette, in press-c) now provide clear indications about the types of help-giver behavior that are likely to have either positive or negative consequences.

Fisher, Nadler, and Whitcher-Alagna (1983) summarized available evidence regarding the types of help-giver behavior that are likely to be responded to in either a positive or negative way. The particular types of help-giver behaviors that are likely to evoke *positive, nondefensive reactions* include positive help-giver attributions toward the help seeker, help giving that limits threats to both the autonomy and self-esteem of the help seeker, and help giving that is accomplished in a cooperative manner. In contrast, help-giver behaviors that are likely to evoke *negative, defensive reactions* include such things as negative help-giver attributions toward the help seeker, threats to help-seeker autonomy, paternalism, and help that restricts behavior freedoms (i.e., choices).

Positive and Negative
Consequences of Help Giving

Dunst and Trivette (in press-c) recently reviewed and integrated the help-seeking literature, with particular emphasis on help-giver behavior that is likely to have either harmful or positive consequences. The major findings from their synthesis of available evidence resulted in nine major conclusions:

1. Help giving may produce learned helplessness if it undermines family competence and control. According to Coates, Renzaglia, and Embree (1983), this is likely to occur when help (a) directly reduces the help seeker's control over life events and reactions to them; (b) prevents or interferes with acquisition of new competencies or reinforces old, maladaptive behavior; (c) interferes with the perceived self-efficacy of the help seeker and conveys a sense that he or she is inferior or incapable of solving problems; and (d) creates situations where credit about successful outcomes is attributed to the help giver rather than the help seeker.

2. Help giving is likely to foster dependencies when help givers, typically professionals as part of client-professional relationships, take relative and in some cases absolute control over the help seeker's fate. This occurs most often in response to help seeking for acute medical or psychological problems. As Merton et al. (1983) wrote:

> [Because] the professional consulted when the client needs help may never [have] seen the client in a state of general well-being, [he or she] can therefore have only an indirect sense of the *client's capabilities and strengths* [italics added]. This limited perspective reinforces the already ingrained tendency for the professional to exercise paternalistic authority. (p.21)

Somewhat ironically, the more "supportive and positive" the paternalistic tendencies, the more likely dependency will occur (Fisher, Nadler, & Whitcher-Alagna, 1983).

3. Help giving is likely to attenuate the help seeker's self-esteem if the help giver conveys a sense that the help seeker is inferior, incompetent, or inadequate, or if the help giver is patronizing toward the help seeker (Fisher, Nadler, & Whitcher-Alagna, 1983). On the other hand, if the help giver conveys a sense of warmth, caring, and worthiness, the help is likely to have positive influences.

4. Help giving is likely to foster a sense of indebtedness if (a) the benefits derived from the help-seeking/help-giving exchange favor the help seeker, (b) the onus of help seeking resides in the person needing aid and assistance, (c) the help giver's behavior is perceived as altruistic, and (d) comparison with others leads the

help seeker to conclude that the help was something for which he or she should be grateful (Greenberg & Westcott, 1983). This often interferes with the recognition of problems or needs and promotes a failure to seek help.

5. Noncontingent help giving, perhaps more than any other aspect of helping relationships, sets the occasion for increased passivity and dependence (Skinner, 1978). *If the help does not require the recipient to acquire effective behavior and thus renders the person helpless or dependent, the immediate needs of the person may be met, but the ability to teach and foster effective behavior are diminished.*

6. Help giving is likely to have harmful consequences if it is unsolicited and only reinforces already negative feelings of self-esteem. Harmful consequences are likely to be greatest when advice or aid is offered by those whom the recipient does not know or does not wish to have advice from (e.g., a meddling neighbor who gives unsolicited child-rearing advice). Not only is the person unlikely to accept the aid, he or she is likely to react negatively to the help giver's efforts to be helpful (Goranson & Berkowitz, 1966).

7. Help giving is likely to elicit negative reactions if there is incongruence or a mismatch between what is sought and what is offered. Among the consequences of incongruent help are that the recipient is less likely either to accept the help or adhere to prescribed regimens (Dunst & Leet, 1987).

8. Offers of help are also likely to have debilitating effects and elicit negative reactions when others see a person's condition as problematic but the person him or herself perceives no problem and has no identified need (Gross & McMullen, 1983). An awareness of need for help is a major determinant of the consequences of helping relationships, and offers of unnecessary help only serve to increase the probability of resentment.

9. Help giving is most likely to be optimally effective if emphasis is placed on building family strengths as a way of fostering acquisition of self-sustaining behavior (Bandura, 1975; Brickman et al., 1982; Stoneman, 1985). "Every family has strengths and, if the emphasis is on supporting strengths rather than rectifying weaknesses, chances for making a difference in the lives of children and families are vastly increased" (Stoneman, 1985, p. 462).

Taken together, our review of the literature uncovered numerous instances in which attempts at being helpful had negative rather than positive effects. Numerous explanations have been advanced for these differential consequences of help-giving acts (DePaulo et al., 1983; Fisher, Nadler, & DePaulo, 1983; Nadler et al., 1983). We find the explanation advanced by Brickman et al. (1982, 1983) most convincing, and when integrated with formulations by Bandura (1977) and Hobbs (1975; Hobbs et al., 1984) it provides a useful framework for explaining why certain types of helping acts have either empowering or usurping consequences.

Helping Models and Empowerment

Brickman and his colleagues (1982, 1983; Karuza, Zevon, Rabinowitz, & Brickman, 1982; Rabinowitz, Karuza, & Zevon, 1984) contend that the extent to which help seeking and help giving are likely to have differential consequences is partly determined by the particular model of helping to which either or both the help giver and help seeker implicitly or explicitly subscribe. Brickman et al. (1982, 1983) describe four helping models (moral, medical, enlightenment, and compensatory) that differ in terms of the extent to which the help seeker is held responsible for causing problems and whether or not he or she is held responsible for solving problems. Each model leads to a specific set of consequences regarding the help seeker's attributions about the agent responsible for observed changes (Bandura, 1977), which in turn is likely to influence various health and well-being outcomes (O'Leary, 1985) depending upon the locus of attributions about causes, solutions, and change. Collectively, the relationships among these components of the helping process may be depicted as:

Helping Model $\rightarrow$ Self-Efficacy $\rightarrow$ Behavior Outcomes.

The helping models are as defined by Brickman et al. (1982, 1983), self-efficacy refers to the locus of attribution about the agent responsible for observed changes, and behavior outcomes refer to combined influences the three sets of attributions (cause, solution, change) have on the help recipient.

Characteristics of Different Helping Models

Table 4-1 shows the specific attributions and outcomes associated with each helping model. We briefly examine the four models and the consequences of each because this examination provides a basis for understanding which model is most likely to be both enabling and empowering. Before doing so, however, we should note that our interest in the individual characteristics of the models is not one of relative effectiveness. Each of the models has a place as part of helping relationships. Rather, our interest lies in the specific characteristics of the models that are most consistent with our definition of empowerment and thus can be used as a basis for enabling a family to become more competent and capable.

Table 4-1.
Four Models of Helping.

Helping Model (Example)	Help Seeker's Responsibility for the Past (Problem/Need)	+	Help Seeker's Responsibility for the Future (Solution)	-->	Help Seeker's Attributions About Self-Efficacy	-->	Examples of Behavior Outcomes
Moral (advice columns)	High		High		High		Loneliness, physical exhaustion
Medical (hospital care)	Low		Low		Low		Passivity, dependency, learned helplessness
Enlightenment (Alcoholics Anonymous)	High		Low		Low		Lowered self-esteem, incompetence, submissive tendencies
Compensatory (CETA)	Low		High		High		Enhanced well-being, internalized locus of control, increased sense of empowerment

Adapted from Brickman et al. (1982) and Bandura (1977).

Moral Model

In the *moral model*, help seekers are responsible both for creating problems and for solving them. According to Brickman et al. (1982), people who see problems and needs from this perspective feel that others are "neither obligated to help (since everyone's troubles are of their own making) nor capable of helping (since everyone must find their own solutions)" (p. 370). If help is offered, it is typically in the form of reminding people that their fate is of their own doing. Under such conditions, one would expect that attributions about self-efficacy would be high and thus suggest that a moral model of helping might be appropriate for enabling and empowering persons. There is, however, danger in employing a moral model as part of helping relationships. A few examples may help illustrate this danger. Take, for example, a victim of rape. In such cases, the victim would be seen as the causal agent responsible for both the raping incident and dealing with the consequences of the event. Similarly, a parent of a handicapped child would be held responsible for causing the handicapping condition as well as be responsible for carrying the burdens associated with rearing the child.

Loneliness, physical exhaustion, and other debilitating consequences are the predicted outcomes of this model. This is the case because (1) the burden of solving problems rests entirely with the help seeker and (2) the model does not sanction one either to request or accept help. Subscribing to this model by either the help seeker or help giver can have devastating effects on the health, well-being, and self-esteem of the recipient. Although any changes in behavior would likely be attributed to self-help efforts, it is clearly not a model that is consistent with our social systems perspective of empowerment.

Medical Model

In the *medical model*, help seekers are responsible for neither their problems nor solutions. Persons who subscribe to this model believe that physical and psychological problems are illnesses, diseases, or aberrations that only experts can fully understand and thus are capable of treating and correcting. Consequently, the help seeker is likely to attribute behavior change to the help giver and not him or herself, and the likelihood of any maintenance of behavior will be diminished considerably. Passivity, dependency, and other forms of helplessness are the major consequences of this helping model because of the low role expectations placed upon the help seeker.

Although the medical model is perhaps best reflected in the practice of medicine, it is only a "special case of a more general set of assumptions about human behavior" (Rabinowitz et al., 1984, p. 80). It is possible to think of many situations in which a help giver (e.g., therapist) might view an individual's problems (e.g., maladaptive behavior) as related not to the person's own doing and see the therapist as responsible for (1) rearranging contingencies, (2) making rewards available only in the presence of the therapist, and (3) controlling behavior in a manner seen as appropriate by the professional. In such cases, the help seeker is likely to ascribe changes in behavior to the help giver and in turn (1) decrease efforts toward self-efficacious behavior (Bandura, 1977), (2) become more dependent on the help giver (Brickman et al., 1982), and (3) even lose the ability to do things they previously did well (Langer & Benevento, 1978). To the extent that a help seeker or help giver or both subscribe to the medical model of helping, one would expect to find behavior change during treatment but very little maintenance of behavior change. This is the case, in part, because the help seeker has come to learn that the help giver and not him or herself is the agent responsible for affecting behavior change (Bandura, 1977).

Enlightenment Model

In the *enlightenment model*, help seekers are responsible for their problems but are not viewed as capable of solving them, at least on their own. The ability to engage actively in self-sustaining behavior is seen as beyond the control of the help seeker, and thus the person's behavior must be shaped and guided by others who continually remind the person of his or her past wrongdoing, and the need to *depend upon* others for maintaining corrective behavior. On the one hand, this model requires people to accept a negative image of themselves because they have no one to blame but themselves for their problem. On the other hand, to improve, they must submit to and follow regimens prescribed by "experts." "Since solutions to problems lie outside the [help seeker], the solution can be maintained only so long as the relationship with the external authority . . . is maintained" (Brickman et al., 1982, p. 374). Moreover, the "more extensive the situational aids for performance, *the greater are the chances that behavior will be ascribed to external factors* [italics added]" (Bandura, 1977, p. 201). Under such conditions, one would expect to find very little maintenance of behavior change. The major consequences of this helping model include lowered self-esteem and a sense of incompetence, guilt, and other intrapersonal attributions that imply a sinful or flawed character.

Compensatory Model

In the *compensatory model*, help seekers are innocent victims of prior experiences and thus are not responsible for their problems but are responsible for solutions. Programs like Head Start and CETA (Comprehensive Educational Training Association) are based substantially on this helping model. On the one hand, this model de-emphasizes attention to the past and consequently reduces the probability of increasing guilt or attenuation of self-esteem. On the other hand, it emphasizes the help seeker's acquisition of self-sustaining behaviors as well as a sense of self-efficacy (Bandura, 1977). Interventions are:

> . . . designed to *empower* [italics added] [help seekers] to deal more effectively with their environment. A . . . therapist who approaches a [help seeker] in the spirit of the compensatory model says to the [help seeker], in effect, "I am your

servant. How can I help you?'' rather than "Do what I say.'' The typical
response of observers who assume the compensatory model is to *mobilize* [ital-
ics added] on behalf of the [help seeker] . . . until the missing resources have
apparently been supplied and the person can (and should) be responsible for his
or her own fate (Brickman et al., 1982, p. 372).

To the extent that interventions promote behavior change and a sense of self-
efficacy, the help seeker is more likely to attribute responsibility for maintaining
change to him or herself, and the success of the intervention should be enhanced
considerably. The major consequences of this helping model include increased
competence and well-being and enhancement of coping abilities.

This brief examination of the four Brickman et al. (1982, 1983) helping models
shows that the medical and enlightenment models are least consistent with the
definition of empowerment provided above and that the compensatory model has
characteristics that are most consistent with our social systems perspective of
empowerment.

Research Evidence
Regarding the Helping Models

There is a burgeoning body of direct and corroborative evidence regarding predictions based on each of the four helping models (Coates et al., 1983; Karuza et al.,
1982) and the direct and indirect effects suggested by the integrated helping
model/self-efficacy attribution framework proposed above (Bandura, 1977, 1982;
Brown, 1979; O'Leary, 1985). Rabinowitz (cited in Karuza et al., 1982), in a study
designed specifically to establish the existence of the four helping models, found
that each of the helping approaches could be differentiated in terms of attributions
about causes for both problems and solutions. The results showed, for example,
that proponents of the moral (Erhard Seminar Training) and enlightenment
(Campus Crusade for Christ) models rated themselves as more responsible for their
problems compared to proponents of either the medical (infirmary patients) or compensatory (CETA workers) models. In contrast, proponents of the moral and compensatory models rated themselves as more responsible for solutions compared to
proponents of either the medical or enlightenment model.

In a study examining the extent to which adherence to certain helping models
affected locus of attributions regarding the agent responsible for observed changes,
Coates et al. (1983) hypothesized that "recipients who hold more strongly to
models that reduce their responsibility for solutions [enlightenment and medical]
will be most likely to respond to help by becoming helpless" (p. 258). Their
findings supported this expectation. Adherence to a model that reduced the help
seeker's responsibility for solving problems was more likely to result in a greater

display of helplessness following help-seeking and help-giving exchanges. Corroborative evidence from studies by Langer and Benevento (1978) and Morrison, Bushell, Hanson, Fentiman, and Holdridge-Crane (1977) bolster these findings. These investigators not only found a greater display of learned helplessness type behaviors in situations where help seekers were made to feel incompetent, but also found a greater degree of dependence on help givers after aid and assistance were provided to them.

The extent to which ascription to certain helping models is related to well-being and health outcomes has been the focus of a number of studies (Karuza et al., 1982). With respect to the four Brickman et al. (1982, 1983) helping models, the findings regarding attributions about causes of problems are equivocal, whereas the findings concerning attributions about solutions are relatively clear-cut. Of relevance to the present discussion, assuming responsibility for solutions to problems has been found to be consistently related to positive affect and enhanced well-being. Additionally, adherence to the enlightenment (and, to a lesser degree, the moral or medical) model has been associated with negative affect, whereas endorsement of the compensatory model has been associated with positive affect.

A considerable body of evidence has been amassed regarding the relationships for solutions to problems and both behavior maintenance and health outcomes (Brickman et al. 1982; O'Leary, 1985). In general, one is less likely to find any maintenance of behavior change in situations in which change is attributed to external agents rather than the help seeker. Additionally, it has generally been found that people who indicate a greater sense of self-efficacy in producing behavior change are more likely to display positive responses.

Taken together, the evidence briefly reviewed here suggests that the different helping models indeed have differential consequences and that application of the compensatory model has the types of effects that are most consistent with predictions derived from our social systems model of empowerment.

A New Perspective of Enablement and Empowerment

We have used the material presented here as well as additional theoretical and empirical evidence collected elsewhere (Dunst, 1986a; Dunst & Trivette, 1987, Dunst & Trivette, in press-a, in press-b, in press-c) as a basis for proposing a new model of helping. The helping model is substantially derived from the Brickman et al. (1982, 1983) description of the compensatory model but includes components that are not explicit characteristics of this helping style.

An Enabling Model of Helping

The proposed helping model de-emphasizes help-seeker responsibility for causing problems and emphasizes help-seeker responsibility for acquisition of competencies necessary to solve problems, meet needs, realize personal projects, or otherwise attain desired goals. We label the helping perspective an *enablement model* to stress the stance that we believe is necessary to increase the likelihood that a person will become empowered. The term "enablement" reflects the underlying rationale of the model, namely, that the help giver creates opportunities for competencies to be acquired or displayed by the help seeker. Help seekers are assumed to be competent or capable of being competent and, when provided opportunities to do so, are able to deal with problems, concerns, demands, aspirations, and so forth more effectively.

The model, to the extent possible, focuses on promotion of growth-producing behaviors rather than treatment of problems or prevention of negative outcomes.[1] Emphasis is placed on promoting and strengthening individual and family functioning by fostering the acquisition of prosocial, self-sustaining, self-efficacious, and other adaptive behaviors. Help seekers are expected to play a major role in deciding what is important to them, what options they will choose to achieve intentions, and what actions they will take in carrying out plans. The help seeker is the essential agent of change; the help giver supports, encourages, and creates opportunities for the help seeker to become competent. The help giver does not mobilize resources on behalf of the help seeker, but rather creates opportunities for the help seeker to acquire competencies that permit him or her to mobilize sources of resources and support necessary to cope, adapt, and grow in response to life's many challenges. Help givers are expected to be positive, see the strengths of help seekers, and assist help seekers to see their potential and capabilities. This is all done in a cooperative, partnership approach that emphasizes joint responsibility between the help seeker and help giver. The goal of this model is to make help seekers better able to deal effectively with future problems, needs, and aspirations, not to make them problem- or trouble-free.

Implication

The phenomenon of help giving and help seeking is a complex psychological and psychosocial event that has multiple antecedents and consequences. When placed within the context of our discussion of needs, resources, and support, the material presented in this chapter has one major, overriding implication: *It is not just an issue of whether needs are met but rather that manner in which mobilization of resources and support occurs that is a major determinant of enabling and empowering families* (Dunst, 1986a; Dunst & Trivette, 1987, in press-c). To be both enabling and empowering in a way that promotes a family's capabilities and competencies, the family must be actively involved in the process of identifying and mobilizing resources to meet its needs, and the help giver must derive gratification and enjoyment in seeing others become capable. We cannot state these conditions any better than how Maple (1977) described them in his book *Shared Decision Making*. He noted that when help givers see themselves as singularly responsible for rescuing families from their troubles:

> . . . the rescuer becomes a star. It is the author's view that your goal as helpers
> is not to learn how to become a star, but rather to help [others] become the
> "star" in some aspects of their lives. (p. 7)

To help families become stars and shine bright is what we mean when we say a family is empowered.

Note

1. Our model, unlike the Brickman et al. (1982, 1983) models, emphasizes promotion over either treatment or prevention. Moreover, our model is couched in proactive rather than reactive terms, which is consistent with our enablement and empowerment philosophy.

Intervention Principles and Operatives: Linking Theory, Research, and Practice

The preceding discussions of needs, resources, support, and help-giving behavior illustrate the complex relationships among these intrafamily and extrafamily factors and how they influence individual and family behavior. The usefulness of all this information, however, is dependent upon the ease with which it can be translated into practice.

Intervention Paradigms

The paradigm that is generally followed when one argues that intervention ought to be based on sound empirical evidence is:

$$(T + R) \rightarrow P,$$

where T = theory, R = research evidence, and P = intervention practices. However, as we have learned more and more about the complexities of family functioning from both our research and clinical experiences, the shortcomings and limitations of this paradigm have become increasingly obvious. The paradigm implies that theory and research should govern or even dictate intervention practices, whereas we believe theory and research should suggest and guide them. Based on the theorizing of Brandtstadter (1980), Bunge (1967), and Reese and Overton (1980), as well as the results of our own work (Dunst & Trivette, in press-a, in press-b), we believe there has been a missing link between theory and research and their implication for practice. We propose a more useful paradigm as follows:

$$(T + R) \rightarrow SO \rightarrow P,$$

where T, R, and P are defined as above and SO = substantive and operative rules and aids for promoting desired effects. "Whereas substantive technologies yield general rules for producing some desired effect, operative technologies supply decision aids for the effective implementation of substantive-technological rules in the concrete action context" (Brandstadter, 1980, p. 15). Substantive rules are the *principles* that derive from theory and research whereas *intervention operatives* are the actions necessary in order to operationalize the principles. More specifically, principles and intervention operatives constitute the smallest number of rules and practices that will produce a desired effect while at the same time reflecting what is known from theory and research.

Four Assessment and Intervention Principles

Four substantive principles are suggested by the material presented in the preceding chapters of the book:

1. To promote positive child, parent, and family functioning, base intervention efforts on family-identified needs, aspirations, and personal projects.
2. To enhance successful efforts toward meeting needs, use existing family functioning style (strengths and capabilities) as a basis for promoting the family's ability to mobilize resources.
3. To ensure the availability and adequacy of resources for meeting needs, place major emphasis on strengthening the family's personal social network as well as promoting utilization of untapped but potential sources of informal aid and assistance.[1]

4. To enhance a family's ability to become more self-sustaining with respect to meeting its needs, employ helping behaviors that promote the family's acquisition and use of competencies and skills necessary to mobilize and secure resources.

Each of these principles states a pragmatic relationship that specifies an *outcome* and the *action* that has the greatest probability of achieving the end or goal. These principles or general rules form the basis of a technological model for linking theory and research to practice (Brandstadter, 1980).

Rationale for the Principles

The first principle states that the greatest impact on child, parent, and family functioning is most likely to occur when interventions are based on the needs, aspirations, and personal projects a family considers important enough to devote its time and energy. This principle is based on evidence that establishes a clear relationship between needs (desires, aspirations, personal projects, etc.) and a number of aspects of family functioning, including well-being and adherence to professionally prescribed regimens. The second principle states that people are more likely to be successful in efforts to achieve projects, reach aspirations, and meet needs if we build on (strengthen and support) the things the family already does well as a basis for mobilizing resources. This principle is derived from evidence regarding the capabilities that constitute family strengths and how family functioning style affects the ability to deal with normative and nonnormative life events as well as promote growth in all family members. The third principle states that informal support networks are a primary source of resources for meeting needs and, to the extent possible, one should build and strengthen natural support systems as a major way of meeting needs. This principle is based on evidence that shows that the most powerful benefits of support are realized if aid and assistance come primarily from informal sources. The fourth principle states that the family's use and acquisition of competencies for mobilizing resources are most likely to occur when professionals employ helping behaviors that create opportunities for family members to display or become better able to meet their needs. This principle is derived from evidence that demonstrates that different ways of helping have differential effects on the help seeker's ability to become more self-sustaining. The remainder of the book is devoted to descriptions of the intervention operatives that are derived from these four substantive principles.

Note

1. We do not intend to imply that all needs can or should be met by informal support sources. The intent of this principle is not to usurp or supplant natural sources of support when they can be mobilized as a way of meeting needs. According to Hobbs et al. (1984), meeting family needs "do[es] not necessarily require the involvement of formal service bureaucracies, but rather [can be accomplished by] helping parents look toward more primary kinds of social support, such as family members, kinship groups, neighbors, and voluntary associations" (p. 50). To the extent that this is possible, it should be the focus of intervention efforts.

6

A Family Systems Assessment and Intervention Model

Our substantive principles suggest that family-level assessment and intervention include (1) specification of family needs, aspirations, and projects, (2) identification of intrafamily strengths and capabilities, (3) identification of sources of support and resources for meeting needs and achieving projects, and (4) proactive staff roles in helping families mobilize resources to meet needs.[1] This four-component model is deceivingly simple and remarkably easy to operationalize.

The model is implemented in the following way:

1. Identify family aspirations and projects using any number of needs-based assessment procedures and strategies to determine the things the family considers important enough to devote time and energy.
2. Identify family strengths and capabilities to emphasize the things the family already does well and determine the particular strengths that increase the likelihood of a family mobilizing resources to meet needs.
3. "Map" the family's personal social network to identify both existing sources of support and resources and untapped but potential sources of aid and assistance.
4. Function in a number of different roles to enable and empower the family to become more competent in mobilizing resources to meet its needs and achieve desired goals.

Table 6–1 shows the correspondence between the substantive principles and these four associated goals.

Learning and Perfecting the Craft

The ability to employ our assessment and intervention process is a *craft* that can be learned and perfected with time and practice. As previously noted, our approach to working with families is best described as a *dynamic, fluid process*. The division of the overall assessment and intervention process into separate components is done primarily for heuristic reasons. Needs and aspirations, family strengths and capabilities, and support and resources are interdependent aspects of family functioning, and the extent to which they are optimally integrated is dependent upon the ways in which the help giver enables and empowers families (see Figure 1–1). In practice, the four components considerably overlap, and the majority of activities within each component are implemented in a parallel and integrated rather than a sequential fashion. Collectively, the operatives within each component define a process that can be used to operationalize the principles in a way that promotes a family's ability to meet needs through mobilization of intrafamily and extrafamily resources.

Learning the craft and using it to enable and empower families requires that help-seeker/help-giver exchanges have certain characteristics if they are to be optimally effective in promoting the abilities of families to meet their needs.[2]

1. The heart of the process for enabling and empowering families is the *relationship* established between the help seeker and help giver. Accordingly, the help giver must develop a relationship with the family in which he or she becomes a trusted confidant. Remember that each and every contact with the family counts toward establishing a help-seeker/help-giver relationship that eventually evolves into a partnership. It is a partnership that creates the medium for effective work with families.
2. Effective *communication* is the name of the game. The principle way to establish partnerships with families is to communicate in a way that treats individual members and the family unit with respect and trust. Emphasis should be placed on active and reflective listening techniques as a way of understanding and supporting families.
3. *Honesty* is the first and foremost requirement of effective communication and partnerships. Each and every interaction with the family must include a clear statement about the purpose of the exchange, what will be asked, and

Table 6-1.

Relationship Between the Four Substantive Principles and Assessment/Intervention Goals.

Substantive Principles	Assessment/Intervention Goals
1. To promote positive child, parent, and family functioning, base intervention efforts on family-identified needs, aspirations, personal projects, and priorities.	Identify family aspirations and projects using needs-based assessment procedures and strategies to determine the things the family considers important enough to devote time and energy.
2. To enhance successful efforts toward meeting needs, use existing family functioning style (strengths and capabilities) as a basis for promoting the family's ability to mobilize resources.	Identify family strengths and capabilities to (a) emphasize the things the family already does well and (b) determine the particular strengths that increase the likelihood of a family mobilizing resources to meet needs.
3. To insure the availability and adequacy of resources for meeting needs, place major emphasis upon strengthening the family's personal social network as well as promoting utilization of untapped but potential sources of informal aid and assistance.	"Map" the family's personal social network to identify both existing sources of support and resources, and untapped but potential sources of aid and assistance.
4. To enhance a family's ability to become more self-sustaining with respect to meeting its needs, employ helping behaviors that promote the family's acquisition and use of competencies and skills necessary to mobilize and secure resources.	Function in a number of different roles to enable and empower the family to become more competent in mobilizing resources to meet its needs and achieve desired goals.

how the information will be used. We have found repeatedly that if one is straightforward and "up front" with families in a way that communicates sincere caring and interest in the well-being of all family members, families will be open and honest in return.

4. Effective help-giving requires *understanding* of families' concerns and interests and not minute details about every aspect of the family's life. By restricting attention to what is important to families (needs, concerns, projects, etc.), information-gathering becomes focused rather than inclusive.

5. Emphasis should be placed upon *solutions* rather than causes. Effective interactions that are both positive and proactive focus on identifying choices and options for meeting needs rather than placing blame or looking for reasons why things are not as they ought to be.

6. Effective help-giving encourages and promotes movement from concerns to needs to *actions* as rapidly as possible. As little time and energy as possible are devoted to problems and negative discussions. Rather, one should create interactive exchanges in which (help-giver) listening promotes (help-seeker) sharing, sharing promotes (help-giver) understanding, understanding promotes (help-seeker and help-giver) exploration, and exploration promotes (help-seeker) action.

7. *Confidentiality* must be maintained and preserved at all times. The help giver must communicate to the help seeker that what is shared during interactions will be held in strictest confidence. If the information is to be shared or discussed with others (e.g., team members), this must be made explicitly clear to the family. It must also be made explicitly clear that no information will be shared with others without the family's permission.

These seven basic but oftentimes forgotten characteristics of effective help giving must be mastered and continually rehearsed if the craft is to be practiced effectively. It would be a good habit for help givers to review these characteristics regularly and ask themselves if their behavior is consistent with these attributes. If the answer is yes, keep up the good work. If the answer is no, take the time to relearn these standards of proactive, effective helping.

A Metaphor for Conceptualizing Family Systems Intervention

As we stated earlier, the process of enabling and empowering families can be thought of as a system of interlocking gears (needs and aspirations, family strengths and capabilities, support and resources) that must be properly aligned if motion and energy are to be passed from one gear to another. Each gear in the system serves a specific function and, when properly adjusted, generates energy and power that make the parts of the whole contribute to optimal efficiency.

The dynamic processes that make up the (family) system can be likened to those on a touring bike where, at any given time, one gear plays a more important role, but it is still the particular alignment among all gears that generates momentum, speed, energy, and power. The alignment of the gears (needs and aspirations, family strengths and capabilities, support and resources) is primarily influenced by two factors: the terrain (developmental course) that is being traversed (by the family) and the capabilities necessary for the family to drive the system forward in a positive direction.

Conceptualizing the interrelationship among needs and aspirations, strengths and capabilities, and resources and support as an interlocking set of gears that forms a system that generates energy and power requires a shift in how help givers work with families. The goal is not for the help giver to take control of the system and define the family's developmental course. Rather, the goal is one of promoting the family's ability to negotiate alignment of the gears of the system in a way that makes it operate as efficiently as possible. We have found it helpful to think of the process of enabling and empowering families as a series of questions that need to be answered in working with families. Table 6–2 includes a list of questions that the help giver might pose to him or herself as part of the assessment and intervention process designed to enable and empower families. These questions are designed as a way of drawing the help giver's attention to important aspects of working with families, as well as serve as a way of self-evaluating his or her own behavior, during interactions with the family.

Identifying Family Needs

The purpose of this component of the assessment and intervention process is to identify both the needs and projects that a family considers important enough to devote its time and energy.

The ability to identify family needs and projects adequately requires us to employ the broader-based needs hierarchy perspective described in Chapter 2. Needs, aspirations, and projects may be thought of as varying along a continuum from basic needs (money, food, shelter, etc.) to enrichment (communication, job, adult education, child-level intervention, etc.) to generativity (sharing experiences with others, security, etc.) Hartman and Laird (1983) and Trivette et al. (1986) both include useful lists of needs hierarchies that can be used as guides for identifying intervention targets. Table 2–1 in Chapter 2 shows a taxonomy of need categories and needs that can be useful for identifying what families may consider important enough to devote their time and energy.

Table 6-2.

Questions for Promoting Implementation of the Assessment and Intervention Process.

Identifying Needs	Identifying Family Functioning Style	Identifying Sources of Support and Resources	Help-Giving Roles and Behavior
1. What are the family's concerns and interests?	1. Do individual family members display commitment toward the well-being of other family members and the family as a whole? In what ways?	1. Who are the people that the family members have contact with on a regular basis or feel close to?	1. Did I create opportunities for the family to share concerns? Did I promote the family's ability to translate concerns into needs?
2. What factors or conditions contribute to the family's concerns and interests?	2. Do individual family members display appreciation for the small and large accomplishments of other family members? How so?	2. What social groups or organizations do the family or individual family members belong to?	2. Did I help the family identify projects and aspirations in a way that promoted a feeling of competence in defining needs?
3. What are the needs and projects that derive from these concerns and interests?	3. Do family members spend time doing things together? In what ways?	3. What agencies or professional organizations do the family or individual family members come in contact with on a regular basis?	3. Did I create opportunities for the family to demonstrate or describe situations that reflected strengths?
4. In which ways does the family define its needs (projects, aspirations, etc.)?	4. Are there family beliefs or values that provide direction to the family's life? What are the beliefs?	4. What types of social support and resources do different people, groups, and agencies provide to the family?	4. Did I emphasize the positive aspects of family functioning? Did I rephrase and re-
5. Is there consensus among family members regarding the importance of the needs?			
6. Are there other concerns or			

interests expressed by individual family members?

7. If there are individualized needs, are other family members supportive and in agreement with the person's appraisal of his own projects or aspirations?

8. Are there apparent reasons why other needs are not currently defined as such by the family?

9. Are there ways of helping the family see its situation differently so needs become more readily apparent?

10. Does the family have the time and energy for meeting needs? If not, why?

11. Does the family see the benefits of devoting time and energy to meet needs?

5. Does the family agree on what needs and projects are important enough to devote its time and energy?

6. Do family members communicate with one another in a way that reflects positive functioning? How?

7. Are there rules and expectations that guide family behavior? What are they?

8. Does the family use a variety of coping strategies that promote positive functioning in dealing with both normal and difficult life events? What are they?

9. Does the family engage in effective problem-solving activities? What are they?

5. How does the family currently mobilize its personal social network to obtain resources?

6. What types of support and resources does the family provide to members of its personal social network?

7. Is provision of support and resources to others by the family viewed by the family as a benefit or burden?

8. Which network members constitute resources for meeting identified needs?

9. Who are potential but underutilized or unidentified sources of support for meeting identified needs?

frame negative comments in a positive manner?

5. Did I create opportunities for the family to identify sources of support for meeting needs and help the family explore ways of procuring these resources?

6. Did I emphasize the use of informal support network members as a primary source of aid and assistance?

7. Did I appropriately make suggestions or point out options for meeting needs? Did I allow the family the final decision regarding whether to accept or reject the advice?

8. Did I offer help that was normative and therefore did not infer deviance or undue variations?

Table 6-2, cont'd.

Questions for Promoting Implementation of the Assessment and Intervention Process.

Identifying Needs	Identifying Family Functioning Style	Identifying Sources of Support and Resources	Help-Giving Roles and Behavior
	10. Does the family see the positive aspects of life, even during crises? In what ways?	10. How willing is the family to initiate a request for help or assistance? Do the the benefits of asking for and accepting help outweigh the costs?	9. Did I offer help that matched the family's appraisal of its needs?
	11. Does the family display flexibility and adaptability in division of labor for meeting needs?	11. Are there particular reasons or factors (e.g., sense of indebtedness) that interfere with procuring necessary resources?	10. Did I offer help and make suggestions that would not cost the family undue amounts of time and energy, and resources?
	12. Does the family use a balance between internal and external family resources for meeting needs? In what ways?	12. Will asking for help create a sense of indebtedness? Can this be prevented?	11. Did I promote the family's ability to identify and mobilize resources in a way that resulted in immediate success?
	13. What anecdotes does the does the family share that reflect different strengths and capabilities?	13. Do network members provide help contingently or non-contingently? Is there a	12. Did I create opportunities for the family to display existing competencies or acquire new competencies as

14. What aspects of the physical and social environment reflect family strengths?

15. What strengths and capabilities are used most often in dealing with daily routines and chores?

16. What are the family's hobbies and interests? In what ways do they reflect strengths?

17. Are there opportunities to help the family rephrase and reframe negative comments in a more positive light?

balance ("give and take") in the exchange of aid and assistance between the family and network members?

14. To what extent does the family feel it can depend on network members in times of need?

15. To what extent is the family satisfied with help that is provided by network members?

part of mobilizing resources to meet needs?

13. Did I employ roles that promoted the family's feelings of competence in actualizing plans to procure resources? Was this done in a way that resulted in the family attributing success to its own actions?

14. Was I positive and proactive in all aspects of interactions with the family? Did I use empathic and responsive listening techniques?

15. Did I create opportunities for the family and myself to function in a partnership for identifying and meeting needs?

16. Did I create opportunities for help provided to the family to be reciprocated?

The Relationship
Between Concerns and Needs

The ability to identify needs adequately requires that one understand both the difference between concerns and needs and the relationship between these terms. As noted in Chapter 2, the need for a resource (need recognition) occurs as a result of some perception of discrepancy between what is and what ought to be. An awareness of the difference between actual states or conditions and what is considered normative or valued is what sets the occasion for need recognition. When we say that a person has an awareness of the difference between what is and what ought to be, we say this person has a *concern*.

A concern is described by any number of terms—worry, problem, dilemma, difficulty, uneasiness, and so forth—just as need is often described by any number of terms—aspiration, project, goal, desire, and so forth. Concerns are the conditions that lead to the perception of discrepancies, whereas need recognition involves the identification of resources required to reduce the discrepancy between what is and what ought to be. The differences and relationship between concerns and needs may be thought of as follows:

1A. Concerns are conditions that lead to a recognition that the difference between what is and what ought to be is sufficiently disparate to warrant attention.

1B. Needs are conditions that lead to a recognition that something (i.e., a resource) will reduce the discrepancy between what is and what ought to be.

2. Concerns produce discrepancies, whereas need recognition and resource procurement (solution identification) reduce discrepancies.

In many instances, families do not explicitly specify what their needs are but rather share their concerns (interests, worries, etc.). The help giver must remain cognizant of the difference between concerns and needs throughout the needs identification process and help the family "translate" concerns into needs. One of the major objectives of needs identification is taking family concerns as they are shared with you, and assisting the family in clarifying these concerns in such a way that the specific resources needed to reduce discrepancies are specified. This process is shown in Figure 6–1. In cases where the family shares concerns rather than specifies its needs, the help giver must promote the family's ability to clarify the concern so that one can define the precise nature of the need and consequently the resource(s) required to meet the need.

According to Maple (1977), the ability to clarify concerns, translate them into needs, and identify options for meeting needs within the context of a partnership requires that one build upon a help seeker's strengths and capabilities. As he noted:

The point is neither partner can begin to identify what approach to take until you have pictured what you want to achieve. A help seeker is often initially focused on confusing problem information. He or she knows what ''they don't want.'' They don't want the existing situation that is troubling them.

This negative focus is frustrating, sometimes freezing the person in a wheel-spinning position. However, if a target or goal can be identified, the person can then mobilize his/her energy to identify his/her own approaches and use suggestions from you, their partner. Your suggestions may be slight modifications of the help seeker's ideas, or the help seeker may modify yours, to add additional approaches. (p. 54)

Resolving the Conflict Between Help-Seeker and Help-Giver Identified Needs

We have until this time avoided *the* major concern and question raised by our emphasis on focusing *all* intervention efforts on family-identified and not help-giver-identified needs. Numerous arguments were made in support of this contention, including the family's rightful role in deciding what is in the best interest of the family, research evidence demonstrating the relationship between needs and family functioning, and the fact that unless there is an indicated need by the family, there is not a concern regardless of what a help giver thinks. Notwithstanding the repeated references to these as well as other arguments, the fact of the matter is many professionals have considerable difficulty with the position that we take in this book. How are we to resolve the conflict between what families and professionals believe ought to be done when there is lack of consensus between the respective parties?

The dilemma that professionals get themselves into when working with families is thinking about things as right or wrong, black or white, night or day. Anytime a professional thinks about things in an either-or fashion, sooner or later the professional will see him or herself as right and the family as wrong and try to convince or even coerce the family into doing what the help giver considers appropriate or right. We describe such situations as *oppositional encounters*. How many of us have seen others or even seen ourselves consider a child to have developmental needs that require intervention when the child's parents did not think there was anything wrong? And how many times have we felt obligated to inform parents that unless they intervened, their child might become more retarded or delayed? And how many times did the parents resist or fail to follow our prescriptions? When we are confronted with these types of situations, we engage in oppositional encounters where there are no winners, only losers.

We cannot think of any better way to illustrate an oppositional encounter as well as its resolution than by way of example. One of us recently encountered a situation in which oppositional encounters abounded, yet resolution was readily apparent.

Figure 6-1.

Difference and Relationships Between Concerns and Needs.

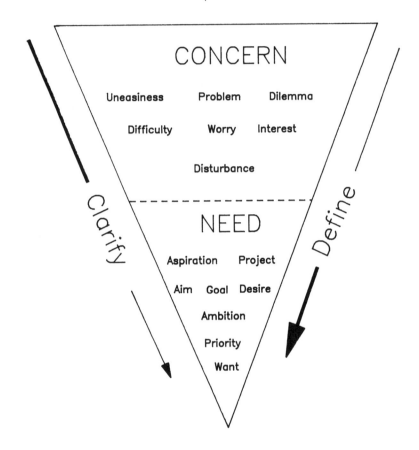

A family with two-year-old twins—"John" and "Jason"—was participating in an early intervention program because John had motor and speech impairments. He was, however, cognitively intact. The mother described John as "sharp as a tack." Jason was developing normally and was a very active, "get-into-everything" boy. John wanted to do everything that Jason did, and the parents were ingenious in devising ways that John could ambulate in order to play with Jason despite his motor difficulties. But therein was the impetus for the oppositional encounter.

The physical therapist strongly recommended that John not be permitted to be in an upright position or ambulate because it promoted poor positioning, and the speech therapist insisted that the mother conduct three half-hour "therapy sessions" with John every day of the week. The mother communicated that any attempt to restrain John from "playing with his brother" made John as well as the rest of the family miserable and that not allowing John to do things that his brother could was a "poor quality of life" for John as well as the rest of the family. Additionally, she noted that John was happiest when he was playing with Jason and was able to learn a tremendous amount from "trying to keep up with his brother." The mother also communicated that with her husband away from home because of his job, and with Jason active and "into everything" all day long, it was impossible to sit John down and carry out prescribed physical and speech therapy activities. "Besides," she commented, "John doesn't enjoy any of the therapy exercises and articulation games, and he cries whenever he senses that I'm going to try to make him do them in the way the therapists want them done." The mother went on to say that she was pleased with the way things were going with John and finally decided that she did not want to follow the prescribed activities. Both therapists, in no uncertain terms, communicated that unless the mother implemented the activities they prescribed, they would refuse to work with John because "it would be just a waste of our time."

What went wrong in this encounter? The answer is quite simple. The therapists saw the situation in an either-or fashion, defining their perspectives as right and the family's as wrong. What could have been done to make this a *supportive* rather than oppositional encounter? The answer is also quite simple and is the main strategy for avoiding conflict.

First, you must start *where the family is*, beginning with the things that are important to the family unit and individual family members (i.e., their needs). In the above case example, it was important to the family that John be able to play with Jason because he was happiest doing so and the family saw play as the context and opportunity for John to learn from Jason. Second, you begin by identifying and pointing out what the child or family does do well within and across different situations or contexts. In our example, one would have noted John's capacity to ambulate, communicate, and socialize in a way that reflected his sense of "happiness." Third, you ask yourself the question, "How can different situations or contexts be used to promote positive changes in individual or family functioning?" Rather than see John's interest in playing with Jason in a negative way, the therapists could have easily asked how John's play and interactions with his brother could be used as the context for enhancing motor and speech abilities. Fourth, you offer suggestions and advice that create opportunities for making slight changes and modifications in the ongoing routines of the family so that the family as a unit or individual family members can display existing or acquire new competencies. John's mother recognized the need for therapy, and if suggestions were made for incorporating therapeutic activities within the ongoing play between John and Jason, the probability of acceptance and implementation of the strategies would have been enhanced considerably. Supportive encounters are obviously the method of choice in working with families.

Methods for Identifying Needs

Needs may be identified either in an interview format or through any number of needs-based assessment scales. Either approach is designed to engage family members in identifying what they *and not others* perceive to be concerns, aspirations, wants, desires, projects, and so forth. *We cannot emphasize enough that identification of family and not professionally-prioritized needs should be the goal of the needs-based assessment process.* Professionals who leave their own agendas outside the assessment process and simply listen to what family members have and want to say will be able to identify what the family views as important and consequently will be able to identify their needs adequately. Stoneman (1985) stated this in the following way: "To be effective [in work with families], service providers must want to hear what parents have to say and must be truly interested in *understanding the family's concerns and needs* [italics added]" (p. 463).

The process we next describe for identifying needs is captured in the following interaction between a mother and help giver:

Mother:	I worry every time somebody in the family gets sick.
Help Giver:	I'm not sure I understand. Can you tell me more?
Mother:	We're never able to see a doctor or get any medicine because we don't have enough money. Getting medical treatment is so expensive, and we don't have health insurance.
Help Giver:	So your concern is that some family member will need medical treatment, but you will not be able to get it because of lack of money or other resources like insurance?
Mother:	That's exactly right! We need a way of getting medical treatment for serious illnesses that we can't treat ourselves.

Interview Procedures

Our experience tells us that a number of considerations should be taken into account when identifying family needs in an interview format. The following operatives, which are summarized in Table 6–3, should be employed to the extent possible when an interview is being used to help a family specify its needs.

- When scheduling the interview, clearly state the purpose of visiting with the family (e.g., "I would like to visit with your family to talk with you further about your concerns and priorities at this time"). Set the occasion for the initial contact to be positive and nonthreatening (e.g., "I want to be as helpful as I can, but exactly what happens and how we proceed will be up to you and your family."). This will help establish the focus of the interview, including what you expect to accomplish, as well as begin the relationship-building process that will eventually determine the success of working with the family. Encourage the family to invite all significant family members to participate in the interview (e.g., "I would like to meet all of the members of your family during my visit, including anyone important to your family, like grandparents, aunts, and cousins. Will you ask everyone to be there?"). This will allow you to observe interactional patterns as well as help you get each family member's perspective on concerns and aspirations. If possible, arrange to conduct the interview in a setting familiar to the family. People tend to be more relaxed and at ease in a familiar context, and you will generally get a better picture of the family when you conduct the interview in such a setting.

- Begin the interview by ascertaining each person's name (including all children present), acknowledging their presence (e.g., thanking them for taking the time to be here), and establishing their relationship with the family. Briefly chat with each person, showing interest in the things they say and share with you. (This information is often subsequently useful in involving the different family members in the interview.) Establishing rapport and placing everyone at ease set the occasion for a successful interview.
- Reiterate both the purpose of the interview and what you expect to accomplish. For example, "From our previous conversation, I have a general idea about your concerns. I would like to talk more about this with you, and hope our time today can be spent helping me better understand your family and child's needs." Make it clear that it is the family's meeting, not yours, and that you are there to learn as much as you can so that you can be of optimal assistance to the family.
- Keep the initial portion of the interview general, and let the family "tell its story" to you. Get the "big picture" of the family, paying particular attention to what each family member perceives as concerns as well as aspirations and to the ways in which the family typically addresses its needs. Remember that your role is to help the family identify and make known its concerns, aspirations, and needs. Keep a running account of the projects, problems, concerns, and needs that the family describes during the course of the interview. Make mental or written notes to be sure that the needs that the family does describe are subsequently addressed in more detail.
- As the big picture of the family begins to emerge, take the concerns that are most important to the family and help them clarify the precise nature of the "projects." Reflect upon what is said, rephrase statements, ask for clarification (e.g., "I know that you want your daughter to walk eventually, but I also hear you saying that it would be helpful if she was able to get

herself from room-to-room right now.''). In many cases, the need for a resource (e.g., money for necessities) may be the result of any number of factors (lack of employment, poor budgeting, etc.) and knowing these factors should guide the types of aid and assistance that are explored as ways of meeting needs. This process often results in a redefinition of a need, and you should be prepared to make adjustments should this occur.

- Throughout the interview, be sensitive and responsive to the verbal and nonverbal messages (tone of voice, body posture, uneasiness, hesitations, etc.) conveyed by all present, and respond and reflect on what you see and hear (e.g., ''You say that you want Bobby to be able to eat more independently, but I sense some hesitancy in your voice. Are you having some doubts about the possibility of this occurring?''). Continue to be an active and reflective listener throughout the interview. The techniques that are most useful include open-ended questions (''What are your feelings or ideas about . . . ?''), leading statements (''Tell me more about . . . ''), and requests for clarification (''Am I understanding you to be saying . . . ?'').

- Conclude the needs-identification portion of the assessment process by restating the needs that have been identified and establishing the order in which they should be addressed. Establish consensus among the family members concerning the needs they identify.

Table 6-3.
Major Operatives for Identifying Family Needs.

- Be positive and proactive in arranging the first contact with the family.

- Take time to establish rapport with the family before beginning the interview.

- Begin by clearly stating the purpose of the interview.

- Encourage the family to share aspirations as well as concerns.

- Help the family clarify concerns, and define the precise nature of their needs.

- Listen empathetically and be responsive throughout the interview.

- Establish consensus regarding the priority needs, projects, etc.

As part of this interview process, one would typically also begin to identify family functioning style as well as to explore options and ways to mobilize resources. The procedures for doing so are described later in this Chapter.

Needs-Based Assessment Scales

Many early intervention professionals, especially those who have not been trained in clinical interviewing techniques, find it difficult and uncomfortable to identify needs and projects in an interview format. An alternative approach is to employ a needs-based, self-report assessment instrument for identifying family projects. Any number of scales are available. They provide a basis for gaining insight about what a family indicates is important and needed. However, our experience tells us that the information obtained from these scales should not be used directly for intervention purposes. Rather, the information should be used as a basis for helping the family clarify and define what they consider important enough to devote time and energy. For example, an assessment tool might evaluate the adequacy of food and shelter. A family that completes the scale indicates that these are needs. One should not base interventions on these responses, but rather use the responses to identify the factors that make these needs, and base the interventions on these factors and not the needs themselves (e.g., "You indicated that you feel you do not have adequate food to feed your family. Can you tell me more about this so I get a better idea about this concern?").

Several steps and considerations should be taken into account when self-report scales are used to assess needs. First, explicitly state why you are asking the family to complete the scale (e.g., "Could you please take the time to fill out this scale about what you might need so that I can be of optimal assistance to you and your family?"). Second, be very clear about how the results will be used (e.g., "After you complete the scale, I'd like us to go over your responses to get a better idea about your concerns and needs."). Third, use the responses to help the family clarify and define what they perceive as a concern or need (e.g., "You indicated that child care is a need. Can you tell me more about what types of child care you feel would be most beneficial?"). Fourth, restate the needs as they are clarified to be sure the family sees your perceptions as accurate (e.g., "If I understand you correctly, you are saying because you will be going back to work, you will need to find day care that is open hours that fit with your work schedule.").

The above process should be repeated for each scale item on which the family indicates it has needs. The interviewer should be as informal as possible while structuring the interpretation of the scale results and the family's responses so that a clear picture of the family's needs, aspirations, and so forth emerges. To the extent possible, one should use the techniques and strategies described above to query the family about its needs. This will help the interviewer gain even more insight into the conditions and factors that influence family-identified needs.

A number of measurement scales are available for assessing family needs (Dunst & Trivette, 1985b; Fewell, 1986). Of them, those with the greatest utility for identifying family-level needs include the Family Needs Survey (Goldfarb, Brotherson, Summers, & Turnbull, 1986; Summers, Turnbull, & Brotherson, 1985), the Parent Needs Inventory (Fewell, Meyer, & Schell, 1981; Robinson & DeRosa, 1980), the Personal Projects Scale (Little, 1983), and selected subscales of the Survey for Parents of Children with Handicaps (Moore, Hamerlynch, Barsh, Spicker, & Jones, 1982). Hartman and Laird (1983), in their book on family systems intervention, describe a needs-based approach to assessment that permits identification of the types of human and physical resources necessary to meet needs (their Chapter 8) as well as propose a series of assessment questions to assist the help giver to structure the problem and the need-identification process (their Chapter 14). We have developed a number of scales specifically for assessment and intervention purposes to help identify family needs. These include the Family Resource Scale (Dunst & Leet, 1987), the Resource Scale for Teenage Mothers (Dunst, Leet, Vance, & Cooper, 1986), the Support Functions Scale (Dunst & Trivette, 1985a), and the Family Needs Scale (Dunst et al., 1985). Copies of these scales are included in Appendix A. Several needs assessment scales are briefly described here to illustrate the ways in which needs can be identified.

Personal Projects Matrix

Little's (1983) Personal Projects Matrix most closely corresponds to the needs-based assessment approach described in this book. A respondent is first asked to list up to ten personal projects that occupy his or her time and energy, and then is asked to rate each of the projects in terms of its importance, enjoyment, difficulty, stress, impact (both positive and negative), and ''progress'' toward meeting the goal (needs, achieving an aspiration, etc.). On the one hand, this assessment system provides a direct way of determining the activities a person considers important enough to devote time and energy. On the other hand, it provides a way of assessing a number of qualitative aspects of the projects with respect to the respondent's perceptions of how the activities impinge upon his or her life. This can be especially useful in determining the extent to which efforts to complete projects will occur.

Family Resource Scale

The Family Resource Scale (FRS) is one instrument that has been developed as part of our work with families. The FRS measures the extent to which different resources are adequate in households with young children. The scale includes 31 items that tap the adequacy of both physical and human resources, including food, shelter, transportation, time to be with family and friends, health care, money to pay bills, child care, and so forth. (A modified version of the FRS is available specifically for teenage mothers; Dunst, Leet, Vance, & Cooper, 1986.) The individual items are roughly ordered from the most to least basic, and the respondent is asked to indicate the extent to which each resource is adequate in his or her family. Each item is rated on a five-point scale ranging from *not at all adequate* to *almost always adequate*. The scale can be completed by a parent or another family member. The FRS can help identify family needs to decide upon the appropriate targets for intervention. Those items rated *not at all adequate* or *seldom adequate* may be taken as evidence that these needs are not being met and provide a basis for exploring with the family what resources are lacking and why they are needed.

Family Needs Scale

The Family Needs Scale (FNS) is similar in format to the FRS but specifically asks family members to indicate the extent of their need for 41 types of resources. The items are organized into nine major categories (financial, food and shelter, employment, communication, etc.), with the items within categories roughly ordered on a continuum from the most to least basic (e.g., the financial resources items range from "Having money to buy necessities" to "Saving money for the future"). Each item is rated on a five-point scale ranging from *almost never (a need)* to *almost always (a need)*. Items rated *sometimes, often,* or *almost always (a need)* may be taken as an indication that those needs are generally unmet, and thus provide a basis for further discussion to pinpoint and define the exact nature of the need.

Support Functions Scale

The Support Functions Scale (SFS) assesses the extent of a person's need for different types of help and assistance. The scale includes 20 items that assess the need for financial (e.g., loans money), emotional (e.g., someone to talk to), instrumental (e.g., child care), and informational (e.g., material describing a handicapping condition) support. Each item is rated on a five-point scale ranging from *never (have a need)* to *quite often (have a need)*. The SFS items and assessment method are based on the results of extensive in-home interviews with over 200 parents of preschool handicapped children in which a taxonomy of needs was generated and subsequently categorized and validated in a series of studies (Dunst & Trivette, 1985a). If the respondent rates an item as *sometimes, often,* or *quite often (have a need)*, this may be taken as an indication that further interviewing (assessment) is necessary to pinpoint the specific help that is needed but lacking.

Component Outcome

The major outcome of the needs-identification portion of the assessment process is a prioritized list of individual and family needs. We have found it most helpful simply to list a family's needs and projects on a Needs by Sources of Support and Resources matrix recording form so that one can visually display the focus of intervention efforts (needs) and then subsequently specify the sources of support and resources that will be mobilized to meet needs. An example of this type of recording form is included in Appendix E. It provides an easy way to keep track of family needs as well as specifying the sources of support for meeting needs.

Identifying Family Functioning Style

The purpose of this component of the assessment and intervention process is to identify a family's individual functioning style in terms of existing intrafamily resources and both strengths and capabilities that can be used to secure additional resources.

Family strengths include the various qualities of strong families described in Chapter 3, including the skills employed in response to demands placed upon the family, the competencies used to mobilize resources, and any other abilities that make the family work well. Family functioning style includes both the strengths and capabilities that constitute resources for meeting needs and the ways in which a family employs strengths and capabilities to secure or create additional resources.

The Family System
and Family Functioning Style

We have found the process of identifying and mobilizing family strengths most beneficial when (1) the family is conceptualized as a system of individual members or subunits displaying capabilities, (2) family strengths are conceptualized as the combination and interaction of resources (capabilities) of individual family members, and (3) family functioning style is conceptualized as the unique clustering and integration of family strengths that promote mobilization of resources to meet needs.

A family system is made up of individual family members, each of whom has personal capabilities and competencies. A family system may be thought of as interconnected individuals (mother, father, children, etc.) who are potential sources of support and resources to one another. The resources that each person possesses are the capabilities and competencies that they have learned and acquired through interactions with others, both within and outside the family unit. The "richness" of a family's reservoir of resources is dependent on the range and variety of competencies of individual family members.

When the family system is conceptualized as an integrated unit comprised of the resources of individual family members, family strengths become the aggregate of the competencies of individual family members either in combination or interaction. By combination we mean two or more family members performing the same or similar tasks to achieve a desired goal (e.g., all family members "chipping in" and cleaning the house before visitors arrive). By interaction, we mean two or more family members performing different tasks to make the family system work in the best interest of individual family members and the family unit as a whole.

By conceptualizing family strengths as integrated and complementary qualities, family functioning style becomes the unique combination and clustering of strengths that promote mobilization of resources to meet family needs. As noted previously, no family possesses all of the strengths specified above but, rather, displays a number of strengths in unique combinations that define the family's particular style of working together to meet needs and achieve aspirations. The following transaction between a mother and help giver suggests strengths that highlight a family's functioning style in mobilizing resources to meet an identified need.

Mother: I'm very worried about my father, who has been admitted to the nursing home. I feel like I should try to spend time with him at least once a week, but I can't take the children.

Help Giver: You were just telling me last week about how your teenage daughter was wanting to earn money for a school trip. Do you think she would be willing to keep the younger children one evening a week so you could visit with your father?

Mother: I hadn't thought about that, but Sandi could care for the children. Just last week, she made their dinner and helped them get their baths when I wasn't feeling well.

Help Giver: I've noticed what a support Sandi has become for you since you and your husband have been separated. Do you think she's mature enough to take on more responsibility for household chores? This might allow you a little more flexibility.

Mother: It's certainly not been easy assuming all responsibility for the children and the running of the house as a single parent. I know Sandi is concerned about her grandfather too. I'll talk with her this afternoon about what we can work out.

Thinking about family functioning style as the combination and interaction of the resources of individual family members as well as the family unit helps make concrete the process of family strengths assessment and intervention. On the one hand, it provides a way of identifying the particular skills and competencies of individual family members as well as identifying the ways in which they are used to address concerns and meet needs. On the other hand, knowledge of individual family member resources, as well as the aggregate of these strengths, provides a basis for the help giver to make suggestions about mobilizing intrafamily resources, as the example above illustrates.

Methods for Identifying Family Functioning Style

Family functioning style may be identified either in an interview format or through any number of family strengths scales. Either approach or a combination of both will identify the things that individual family members and the family unit "do well" and thus constitute intrafamily resources. In the use of either approach, one should remain aware that family functioning style includes both the presence of strengths and capabilities and the manner in which these competencies are used to secure or create resources. One should answer three questions with respect to family functioning style:

1. Which of the 12 qualities of strong families described in Chapter 3 are displayed by the family?
2. How are the strengths used as intrafamily resources for meeting needs?
3. How does the family use these as well as any other capabilities to mobilize or create extrafamily resources to meet needs?

As noted by Stoneman (1985), "Every family has strengths and, if the emphasis is on supporting strengths rather than rectifying weaknesses, chances for making a difference in the lives of children and families are vastly increased" (p. 462).

Interview Procedures

The identification of family strengths as part of the needs-based interview process described above requires one to pay particular attention to both individual family member behavior and interactions among family members. One may also pose questions that elicit descriptions of the things the family does that are indicative of different strengths, capabilities, and intrafamily resources. Table 6-4 summarizes

Table 6-4.
Major Operatives for Identifying Family Functioning Style.

- Focus on the positive aspects of family functioning.

- Pay particular attention to anecdotes shared by the family.

- Comment on those aspects of the physical and social environment that reflect strengths.

- Ask the family to describe the ways in which they deal with daily routines.

- Ask the family about hobbies, interests, etc.

- Rephrase and reframe negative comments in a positive manner.

- Emphasize the positive aspects of family functioning throughout the interview.

What follows are several considerations and strategies that we have found most helpful in identifying family strengths.

- The major sources for identifying family functioning style are the descriptions, behaviors, and interactional patterns displayed by the family during the course of the interview. People rarely name their strengths and capabilities explicitly. Rather, they generally *demonstrate* and *describe* strengths and capabilities by way of example (e.g., "When my wife has to be at the hospital with Johnny, we all pitch in to do whatever needs to get done around the house.") The interviewer should note the various behaviors that a family displays during the interview and determine to what extent these behaviors reflect appreciation for one another, involvement and commitment to family projects, a shared sense of purpose, and other family strength qualities.

- As part of getting a family to "tell its story" to you during the needs-based portion of the assessment process, pay particular attention to the various anecdotes and incidents the family shares with you. These accounts generally include numerous examples of behaviors that reflect strengths and capabilities as well as the ways the family employs intrafamily resources to meet needs.

- Another way to identify family strengths is to observe and take notice of the family's physical environment and use the things the family takes for granted as a way of identifying its capabilities. Are the children safely occupied? (''You always have interesting toys and activities for the children.'') Are there homemade crafts located throughout the house? (''You have a real skill in needlework, and your framed pieces around the house really add a nice touch.'') Is there a vegetable or flower garden? (''I'm sure you must enjoy the fresh vegetables you get from your garden and the savings you have on your grocery bill.'') Is there the smell of home cooked meals? (''Your homemade breads and desserts must make your family feel really special.'') These observations provide a concrete basis for the interviewer to comment on the family's strengths and capabilities, and such occurrences can be used to obtain information about intrafamily resources.

- One of the best ways to get a family to make known its functioning style is to ask its members to describe the daily activities and routines they engage in, and the things they do to ''get through the day.'' (''Can you tell me more about mealtimes. Who generally prepares the meals? Do other family members help out by watching the younger children? Do you find that dinner is an enjoyable event?'') Pay particular attention to the ways in which the family deals and copes with both enjoyable as well as difficult tasks. These ''ways of coping'' are one set of intrafamily resources and constitute the ways a family uses its resources to meet daily needs.

- In addition to the strategies described above, you can ask specific questions designed to elicit descriptions of family strengths and capabilities. (''What are your favorite things to do together?'', ''Do you have any hobbies or interests that you enjoy or find relaxing?'', ''What do you and your children do that you find the most fun?'') Questions like these set the occasion for a family to talk about the things that reflect strengths and capabilities.

- Many families who describe concerns and dilemmas focus on the negative aspects of family functioning (e.g., ''We never seem to be able to get ahead financially.''). Remember that there is always an alternative way of viewing things, and by restating and reframing a problem or concern in a more positive way, you may help the family see the ways in which things are working well (e.g., ''It's really nice the way you are willing to help out with some of your mother's expenses. You must feel good that you are able to be of help to her.''). Throughout the interview, rephrase, restate, and reframe what family members say to emphasize the healthy and positive aspects of family functioning style.

- Many families, particularly those characterized as having long histories of problems and failures, are rarely asked about the ''good things'' that characterize their families. All families have strengths, and by pointing out and commenting on what the family does do well, you can begin to help the family recognize its capabilities (e.g., ''Although you have many demands on you right now, your willingness to do things together seems to have provided you with some 'good' times in the midst of your difficulties.'').

The ability to discern family functioning style can be a major asset in helping families mobilize resources for meeting needs. Awareness of family strengths and the ways in which they are collectively used to cope with life events as well as to promote growth and development provides a basis for strengthening the things the family already does well.

Family Strength Scales

Identification of family functioning style may also be accomplished using any number of self-report, family strengths scales. The Family Strengths Inventory (Stinnett & DeFrain, 1985b), the Family Strengths Scale (Olson, Larsen, & McCubbin, 1983), the Family Functioning Style Scale (Deal, Trivette, & Dunst, 1987), and the Family Strength Questionnaire (Otto, 1975) assess many of the qualities that have been identified as family strengths and capabilities. Each of these scales provides a basis for assessing the degree to which a family is characterized by different qualities and capabilities (e.g., family members respect one another).

As was true for needs-based assessment tools, the responses on self-report, family strength measures should not be viewed as the goal, but rather used for further discussion with the family about the meaning of the responses. For example, a family member might indicate that the ability to communicate is a strength in his or her household. This response should be used to pinpoint how the family communicates, the ways in which communication occurs, etc., to discern the specific behaviors that make this strength an intrafamily resource.

Additionally, it must be continually remembered that not all families will display all the qualities that represent family strengths, and that it is the unique combination of qualities that defines family functioning style. As noted by Otto (1962), ''strengths are not isolated variables, but form clusters and constellations which are *dynamic, fluid, interrelated, and interacting* [italics added]'' (p. 80). The use of family strengths scales should focus primarily on the interrelatedness of different qualities and how qualities are employed in daily living as intrafamily resources and as a way of procuring extrafamily resources. The latter should be the major emphasis of using family strengths scales.

Family Strengths Inventory

The Family Strengths Inventory includes 13 items that measure six major qualities of strong families and a number of aspects of interpersonal and intrapersonal relationships. Each item is rated on a five-point scale based on the degree to which the quality or characteristic is present in the respondent's family. The scale yields a total score that provides a basis for determining overall family strengths. However, it is the individual responses to the 13 scale items that are most useful for determining family functioning style. For example, a respondent might indicate that in his or her family it is very characteristic for them to deal with crises in a positive manner. This would be used to query the respondent about the manner in which this occurs (e.g., "You indicated that your family generally deals with difficult situations in a positive way. Can you tell me about the ways in which you approach or deal with crises that helps you see 'good' even in times of difficulty?"). The response to the question gives the interviewer a better idea about how this quality contributes to an overall family functioning style.

Family Strengths Scale

The Family Strengths Scale includes 12 items that assess two dimensions of family functioning: *family pride* (loyalty, optimism, trust in the family) and *family accord* (ability to accomplish tasks, deal with problems, get along together). For each item, the respondent indicates the extent to which the quality is present in his or her family. The items tap strengths such as trust and confidence, ability to express feelings, congruence in values and beliefs, respect, etc. Responses on individual items as well as subscale scores can be used to ask families why they consider particular characteristics family strengths (e.g., "Could you tell me about how your family prevents problems from re-occurring in your household?"). The response to this question will provide considerable insight into the family's unique functioning style.

Family Functioning Style Scale

The Family Functioning Style Scale assesses all 12 qualities of strong families described in Chapter 3. (A copy of the scale is included in Appendix C.) We developed the scale specifically to assess the extent to which a person believes his or her family is characterized by different strengths and capabilities. The individual scale items are rated on a five-point scale based on the extent to which different statements are true for the respondent's household. The scale items are organized into three major categories of the family strengths: family identity, information sharing, and coping/resource mobilization. As was the case for the other family strengths scales, the responses to individual items are used to probe the family about what they do to communicate, cope, etc.

Component Outcome

The major outcomes of identifying family functioning style are a list of behavior exemplars that reflect the family's strengths and capabilities, and examples of the ways in which intrafamily resources are used both for meeting needs and mobilizing and creating extrafamily resources. These outcomes can easily be accomplished using a recording form that includes space for listing different family behaviors described or displayed during the interview and for indicating whether the behaviors reflect (1) one or more of the 12 qualities of strong families and (2) intrafamily resources for meeting needs or intrafamily resources that are used to procure extrafamily resources, or both. A form that can be used for this purpose is included in Appendix F.

Identifying Sources of Support and Resources

The purpose of this component of the assessment and intervention process model is to identify existing sources of intrafamily and extrafamily support and untapped but potential sources of aid and assistance that match family-identified needs.

Support refers to emotional, physical, informational, and instrumental resources and includes such varied things as someone to talk to about the difficulties of rearing a young child, medical care, information about a particular handicapping condition, transportation provided by a friend, day care, etc. Sources of support may be thought of as varying along a continuum beginning with the family unit and moving outward and progressively more distant from individual family members (Bronfenbrenner, 1979). In our work on explicating the major sources of support potentially available to families, we have been able to discern seven major social units and groups (Dunst, 1985) that can be organized into four major categories (see Figure 6−2). Table 6−5 lists the support sources and includes examples of the people, groups, and agencies who are members of each social unit. These include the nuclear or immediate family (children, parents, other household members), relatives and kin (blood and marriage relatives), informal network members (friends, neighbors, co-workers, etc.), social organizations (church, clubs, etc.), generic professionals and agencies (family/child's physician, health department, public schools, day-care centers, etc.), specialized professional services (early intervention program, specialized clinics, therapists, clinicians, etc.), and policy-making groups and individuals (agency directors, school boards, county and state governments, etc.).

A number of qualitative features of support have been found to be important factors influencing the likelihood of mobilization of resources for meeting needs (see Table 6−6).[3] Which features tend to be most important vary from family to family and from need to need because of situation-specific considerations. How-

Figure 6-2.

Ecological Mapping of the Child and Family
Embedded Within Other Social Systems.

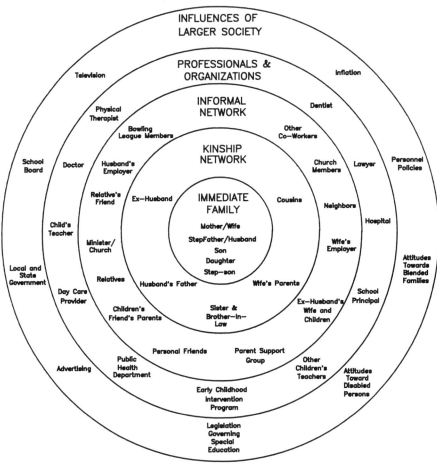

ever, one will generally find that most features apply to most families but differ
with respect to which ones are the most important considerations for a particular
family.

The procedures for identifying and mobilizing sources of support as well as the
ways in which different qualitative features of support influence decisions to seek
and accept help are illustrated in the following transaction:

Parent: I'm dreading the start of the new school year. All of the children
                     need clothes, but I have no money to spare for clothes at this time.

Help Giver: How have you gotten clothes for the children in the past?

Parent: Sometimes I've been able to find some nice second-hand clothes at garage or yard sales.

Help Giver: Do you have any family members or friends with children that you could ask about some clothes?

Parent: A friend of mine through church has children a little older than mine, but I don't know what she does with the clothes they've outgrown. I wouldn't want to ask her without offering to pay for them.

Help Giver: Can you think of something you could offer in exchange for some clothes—baby sitting or some of your delicious baked goods?

Table 6-5.
Major Sources of Support Available for Meeting Family Needs.

Support Sources	Members
Nuclear family	Spouse/partner, children, other household members
Kinship	Blood and marriage relatives
Informal network	Friends, neighbors, church associates, co-workers, etc.
Social organizations	Church, service clubs, etc.
Generic professionals	Family physician, hospital, day care centers, schools, etc.
Specialized professionals	Early intervention programs, speech and physical therapists, infant specialists, etc.
Policy makers	Agency directors, school boards, city councils, state representatives, etc.

Parent: I know she's always looking for someone to baby sit. She's taking some night courses at the local college. I'll give her a call and see if she would be interested in arranging an exchange.

One week later:

Parent: I talked to my friend and she exchanged some clothes for me baby sitting for her. I'm so relieved that the children have something nice to wear to school, and am pleased that my friend was so willing and enthused about me baby sitting her children.

Table 6-6.
Five Qualitative Features
of Help-Seeking/Help-Giving Exchanges.

Qualitative Features	Definitions
Response costs	Extent to which the costs of seeking and accepting help do not outweigh the benefits
Dependability	Extent to which the family can depend on network members in times of need and how willing network members are in terms of providing aid and assistance
Indebtedness	Extent to which help giving by network members creates a personal or psychological sense of obligation
Reciprocity	Extent to which exchange of favors is sanctioned and approved but not expected
Satisfaction	Extent to which one is satisfied with help that is provided by network members

Methods for Identifying Support and Resources

The process of identifying both existing sources of support and potential-but-untapped sources of resources and assistance can be accomplished either in an interview format or through use of self-report or clinically administered social support scales (Dunst & Trivette, 1985b; Fewell, 1986). Either approach, or a combination of both, is designed to identify sources of aid and assistance and the types of resources that the family can use to meet its needs.

Interview Procedures

Identifying sources of support and resources for meeting family needs in an interview format requires a proactive role on the part of the interviewer. Indeed, the help giver must engage in a number of different roles (see below) to help families identify existing sources of support, recognize additional options for meeting needs, and link the families with these resources. Our experience tells us that a number of considerations should be taken into account as part of helping families identify and mobilize their support networks (see Table 6–7). The following are the operatives that we have found most helpful in identifying sources of support and resources for meeting needs.

- Start by having the family generate a preliminary list of persons, social organizations, and agencies that they have contact with on a regular basis or that they contact in response to specific concerns or problems. These individuals and groups represent the family's personal social network. Explain to the family that many of the resources that each of us needs are often available from a number of sources. By "mapping" their personal networks, it will be possible to identify which sources of support may have resources necessary for meeting their needs.

- One of the simplest yet most effective strategies for promoting use of existing as well as potential sources of support is to query the family about what has already been done and whether family members have thought about other ways of meeting their needs. Questions like "Who have you already talked to about ... ?", "What are you currently doing to handle this need?", and "Have you thought about ... as a way of getting that resource?" set the occasion not only for identifying sources of support and resources but also discussing the ways in which the family goes about mobilizing its personal social networks.

- Beginning with the priority project identified as part of the needs-based portion of the assessment and intervention process, explore with the family the extent to which existing network members, including individual family members, have the necessary resources for meeting the need. It is important to remember that the family unit is often a major source of aid and assistance and, to the extent possible, intrafamily resources should be explored as options for meeting needs. Once the sources of resources for meeting the priority need have been identified, repeat the process for the next family-identified need. Continue until the family is able to engage in the process of matching resources to needs.

- For those needs that cannot be met by existing network members, explore with the family untapped but potential sources of aid and assistance that might represent viable options. One major role that you can and should play is to suggest and discuss resources you are familiar with that are not identified as sources of support by the family. For example, a family might not see another parent as someone who can provide information about his or her child's handicapping condition, whereas you may know a person who is knowledgeable about this condition. In such a case, you might raise the possibility that this person could be contacted and might be willing to talk to the family about its concerns.

- Existing sources of support are oftentimes not seen as viable options for meeting needs because other needs interfere with accessing resources (e.g., a parent may desire a day-care placement for his or her child but does not see this as a possibility because the school does not provide transportation). In such instances, you can help the family explore ways to obtain the additional resources that will permit the family-identified need to be met (e.g., arranging for a family already transporting their own child to the day-care center to provide transportation in exchange for child care in the evenings or on weekends).

- The extent to which a family sees existing and potential social network members as having resources necessary to meet needs is often dependent upon a host of factors, including the response costs involved in asking for help, the dependability of network members, and the sense of indebtedness the family is likely to feel as a result of accepting help (see Table 6-6). It is important when identifying network members who represent options for meeting needs to obtain some indication of how the family feels about asking for help, and how the family perceives others' response to being asked for help. This will allow not only identification of factors that promote or impede procurement of resources, but will also provide a vehicle for exploring ways to deal with obstacles for mobilizing resources.

- Once existing and potential sources of support are identified, you and the family should work out the necessary plans to help the family mobilize the resources in a manner that builds on existing capabilities and thus further strengthens family functioning. To the extent possible, plans to access help or assistance should be made contingent upon families playing an active role in carrying out the courses of action. Noncontingent helping only postpones the acquisition of effective behavior and increases the probability of creating a dependency on professionals.

- With respect to options for meeting needs, *the focus of all efforts to meet needs should be the mobilization of informal support networks at the level closest to the family unit* to the extent that individuals or groups have or can generate the resources necessary to meet individual family needs. A rule of thumb that we believe should be followed in working with families is never to use or create a professional resource or service as a way of meeting needs if the resource can be provided by members of the family's informal social network. This strategy insures that formal support does not replace or supplant informal support networks but rather strengthens them through mobilization of linkages that permits needs to be met. Consequently, you should strive to provide only those professional services that cannot be provided by informal socializing agents.

- Create the opportunity for the family to actualize plans for mobilizing resources using enabling experiences. Encourage and support the family in a way that promotes and strengthens its ability to display or acquire competencies necessary to procure resources for meeting needs. Enabling experiences include any means or opportunity to observe, learn from, and interact with others (including you) in a way that provides an occasion to share knowledge or skills.

The process of identifying sources of support, matching resources with needs, and assessing the ways in which different characteristics of help-seeker and help-giver exchanges influence decisions about asking and accepting help is itself a form of intervention. The process also sets the occasion for promoting the use and acquisition of skills and competencies necessary for the family to mobilize its social support network. To the extent that this is done in a proactive way, actualizing the plan should have positive influences on parent, family, and child functioning.

Social Support Scales

There are numerous scales available that are specifically designed to assess one or more components of the social support domain (Cohen & Syme, 1985a; Dunst & Trivette, 1985b; Fewell, 1986). These scales can aid in the identification of a family's existing support network as well as provide a basis for exploring the characteristics of help-seeking and help-giving exchanges that promote or impede mobilization of resources.

The use of self-report or clinically administered social support scales can provide information for further discussion with the family about which sources of support are most and least helpful, which sources are options for meeting needs, how the family feels about asking for help, how the family thinks people will respond to being asked for help, etc. The network-mapping process together with queries about the family's qualitative assessment of its social network is a simple yet highly efficient process for matching resources with needs. Our experience tells us that the process of identifying and evaluating the usefulness of different sources of support for meeting needs, although simple and efficient, does require that one be sensitive to the verbal and nonverbal behavior of the family when matching

Table 6-7.
Major Operatives for Identifying
Sources of Support and Resources for Meeting Needs.

- Identify the members of the family's personal social network.

- Employ probing techniques to identify how the family mobilizes resources from network members.

- Determine which network members might constitute "options" for meeting identified but unmet needs.

- Explore potential but currently untapped sources of aid and assistance for meeting needs.

- Explore ways in which needs are unmet because of other unmet needs.

- Be sensitive and responsive to the various qualitative aspects of support exchanges throughout the interview.

- Jointly develop plans for mobilizing resources with the family.

- Emphasize use of informal support as a way of meeting needs.

- Promote the family's ability to display or acquire competencies for meeting needs.

resources to needs. This is especially true in terms of willingness to seek and ask for help and willingness of different network members to provide aid and assistance. Therefore, one should be sensitive to how the family responds to different options for meeting needs, and use the response as a basis for prompting clarification (e.g., "You indicated that your aunt might be able to provide transportation to get your child therapy, but I sense that you are hesitant about asking her. Is there some reason why you feel this way?"). This type of follow-up probe helps the family clarify its reasons for not wanting to ask for assistance as well as provides a basis for exploring ways of making the particular source of support a viable option or exploring alternative options. One should not assume that because a network member has a resource that a family could use to meet a need that it automatically means this is an appropriate source of support to the family. Concerns about helpfulness, dependability, willingness, reciprocity, indebtedness, response costs, etc. need to be explored and examined if there is any reservation about using any particular sources of support to meet needs (see Table 6–6).

We have developed a number of scales that measure different aspects of social support and thus have utility for identifying existing and potential sources of support for meeting family needs. These include the Family Support Scale (Dunst et al., 1984), the Inventory of Social Support (Trivette & Dunst, 1986), and the Personal Network Matrix (Trivette & Dunst, 1987b). Copies of the scales are included in Appendix B. In addition, we find both the Psychosocial Kinship Inventory (Pattison, DeFrancisco, Wood, Frazier, & Crowder, 1975) and the Perceived Support Network Inventory (Oritt, Paul, & Behrman, 1985) of particular clinical value because of the format they use for identifying different aspects of a family's personal social network. These scales as well as instruments that we have developed are briefly described next.

Psychosocial Kinship Inventory

The Psychosocial Kinship Inventory can be particularly helpful in assessing various aspects of a person's social network. The scale includes procedures for both identifying the members of the person's personal network and for assessing 11 separate dimensions of support for each network member. The 11 dimensions include *kind* of feelings and thoughts toward the respondent's social support members, *strength* of these feelings and thoughts, *help* provided by these network members, degree of *emotional support* they provide, frequency of *contact* with them, degree of *stability* of the relationships, physical *proximity* to the network members, *kind* of feelings and thoughts believed held toward the respondent by the network members, *strength* of feelings believed held toward the respondents, *help* provided to kinship members, and *emotional support* provided to these kinship members. Each of these dimensions are rated on a five-point scale for each person listed by the respondent. The results generate a nice picture of the person's social network and provide a basis for exploring which network members are used for meeting needs and which network members represent potential but untapped sources of aid and assistance.

Perceived Support Network Inventory

The Perceived Support Network Inventory (SNI) is a particularly useful instrument because of its multidimensional format. It provides an objective way of determining the members of a family's personal network, the relationships with these people, the types of support they provide, and the manner in which support is provided, as well as the extent to which the family is satisfied with support. The respondent is first asked to list all the people he or she would ordinarily go to for help or assistance. Second, the respondent indicates what types of support they would generally seek from these people. Third, the person then rates a number of qualitative aspects of support exchanges. The SNI, although developed for research purposes, does have utility as part of measuring many of the aspects of a family's social support network that have been found to influence decisions about seeking and accepting help.

Family Support Scale

The Family Support Scale (FSS) is an 18 – item (plus 2 self-initiated items) self-report measure that assesses the degree to which different support sources are helpful to families rearing a young child. The sources of support include the respondent's own parents, spouse or partner, friends, neighbors, co-workers, church, professionals, and social groups and organizations. Each item is rated on a five-point scale ranging from *not at all helpful* to *extremely helpful*. The results from the FSS can be used to query persons about members of their social network, including who is helpful and why, who is not helpful and why, which sources of support are used and not used and why, etc.

Inventory of Social Support

The Inventory of Social Support (ISS) provides a basis for both mapping a person's social network and assessing the extent to which identified needs are being met by members of the individual's support network. The ISS is used in conjunction with the Support Functions Scale described above (also see Appendix A). The scale is divided into two parts: identification of (1) family needs and (2) support sources to meet those needs. The taxonomy of needs is identical to that on the short form of the Support Functions Scale; however, respondents indicate who in their network provides the particular types of support rather than indicating if they need the various types of aid and assistance. Nineteen potential sources of support are included on the scale, ranging from intrafamily (spouse/partner, children, etc.) to informal (friends, relatives, church, etc.) to formal (day care, physicians, human service agencies, etc.) support sources. The scale is organized in a matrix format with the needs listed down the left-hand column and the sources of support displayed across the top. Respondents are asked to read each needs question (e.g., "Who encourages you or keeps you going when things seem hard?") and then indicate who in their support network provides help or assistance with this type of need. The scale can be completed in either a self-report or interview format.

A completed matrix provides a visual display of who functions as a source of support to the respondent and what types of support they provide. The information can then be used to explore the manner in which a family can mobilize its support network to meet identified needs. This is accomplished in conjunction with the findings from the Support Functions Scale in the following manner. If a respondent indicates no need for a particular type of support on the Support Functions Scale and few or no individuals or groups provide that type of support, one should not be concerned since this type of aid and assistance is not needed (at least at that time). If a respondent indicates a need for a particular type of support and that this need is being adequately addressed by, say, four support sources, one should also not be concerned to the extent that the person indicates verbally or nonverbally that "things are going well" or "everything is OK." However, if the respondent indicates that he or she has a need but few or no support sources provide help or assistance in this area, the incongruence may be taken as an indication for further interviewing to specify the need more precisely and explore ways of getting the family to learn to use its social network to access needed resources and support.

Personal Network Matrix

The Personal Network Matrix (PNM) is modeled after the Inventory of Social Support (ISS) and is designed to map a person's social network in terms of those network members who are currently providing aid and assistance to meet individually identified needs. The PNM includes the same sources of support included on the ISS (as well as space to add other network members). Instead of preselected categories of needs, the PNM provides space to list those needs identified as part of the needs-identification component of the assessment and intervention process. The person completing the scale indicates, for all of the support sources listed, the ones currently being used for meeting needs as well as marks potential but untapped sources of support. Additionally, the respondent indicates the extent to which he or she perceives network members as willing to provide aid and assistance and the extent to which he or she perceives it to be worth the time and effort to ask or seek help from those identified as potential sources of aid and assistance. A completed matrix and the qualitative ratings provide a basis for understanding the dynamics of the person's social network and exploring ways of mobilizing resources for meeting needs.

Component Outcome

The major outcome of "mapping" a family's personal social network is the identification of viable sources of support that can be used for matching resources with needs as well as a complete understanding of the conditions that are likely to promote or interfere with asking and accepting help and assistance. The particular sources of support that are identified as viable options can be placed on the Needs by Sources of Support and Resources matrix recording form described above (see Appendix E). Completion of the support identification portion of the assessment and intervention process provides a nice visual summary of what resources are needed and the sources of support that will be employed for mobilizing them.

Help-Giver Roles
and Help-Giving Behavior

The purpose of this component of the assessment and intervention process is to employ helping behaviors that enable families to maximize the use of their existing competencies and empower families with new competencies that make them more self-sustaining in terms of mobilizing resources to meet needs.

The ability to attain this goal is guided by a proactive approach to working with families, a shift and expansion in the roles help givers employ in working with families, and a set of guidelines that can be used to enable and empower families. In contrast to the previous three components of the process which emphasize assessment of different aspects of the family, the focus of this component is the ways in which help givers work with families so that the latter can become more competent and self-sustaining with respect to their ability to mobilize resources for meeting needs.

The implementation of our assessment and intervention model is guided by a number of beliefs that emphasize a proactive, highly responsive approach to working with families. First, major emphasis is placed on both *enabling and empowering* families (Dunst, 1986a; Dunst & Trivette, 1987). As already discussed, enabling families means creating opportunities for family members to become more competent, independent, and self-sustaining with respect to their abilities to mobilize their social networks to get needs met and attain desired goals. Empowering families means carrying out interventions in a manner in which family members acquire a sense of control over their lives as a result of their efforts to meet their needs. Second, major emphasis is placed on *strengthening* families and their natural support networks and neither usurping decision-making nor supplanting their support networks with professional services (Hobbs et al., 1984). Strengthening families means supporting and building upon the things the family already does well as a basis for promoting and encouraging the mobilization of resources among the family's network members. Third, major emphasis is placed on enhancing families' acquisition of a wide variety of *competencies* that permit them to become capable of meeting needs through mobilization of their support networks (Wikler & Keenan, 1983). Enhancing the acquisition of competencies means providing families with the information and skills necessary for them to become more self-sustaining and better able to promote personal well-being as well as have positive influences in other areas of family functioning (Dunst, 1985; Dunst & Trivette, in press-a).

The ability to enable, empower, and strengthen families as well as foster acquisition of needed competencies requires a shift in the roles help givers typically employ in working with families, as well as a unique style of interaction as part of enacting these roles. These various aspects of help- seeking and help-giving exchanges are illustrated in the following transaction:

Parent: I have to return to work full time to retain my health insurance so that I am able to pay our monthly bills, but finding a baby sitter has me worried.

Help Giver: Can you tell me what type of child care arrangement you have in mind? A private sitter or day care?

Parent: I really would like to find an individual to keep the baby in her home, but I don't know anyone and I don't have much time to look for someone! There's also the issue of having to tube feed the baby and finding someone willing to do that!

Help Giver: I can tell by your voice that you're really anxious about this. Let's look at some ways you might go about finding a sitter. Since your preference is having child care in the home of an individual, let's start by looking at how you might find someone. Is there someone in your family or a friend or neighbor who might know of an individual who keeps children? What about some of the people you work with who have children?

Parent: My sister-in-law uses a sitter who keeps her child part time. Judy, a friend of mine at work, takes her children to an individual's home and she is pleased with her.

Help Giver: So there are two people you know who use private sitters. Can you check with them about getting the names and telephone numbers of the sitters and any other potential sitters they might know?

Parent:	Yes, I guess so. But how will I know if these sitters are reliable and if I can trust them with my baby?
Help Giver:	I know it's going to be difficult for you to have your baby in the care of someone else. You've been her primary care provider since birth, and this will mean an adjustment for both of you.
Parent:	I can't tell you how much I've agonized over this and have tried to look at how we could manage without my salary, but there just doesn't seem to be any way without returning to work.
Help Giver:	Separating from the baby will not be easy, but there are some things you can do that will help you choose a sitter so that you have confidence in the person from the outset.
Parent:	I certainly want to visit the home of anyone I am considering and talk with her. I don't want to take someone else's word on how she might be.
Help Giver:	That's definitely a good idea, although you might also get references from other parents who have used the sitters you are considering. Do you have in mind what you are going to look for or ask when you visit potential sitters?
Parent:	I know I want a place that's clean and safe for children. I also want someone who will love her and spend time with her rather than leave her in the crib.
Help Giver:	I agree that both of those points are very important. You might spend some time thinking of some other questions you would ask and writing them down to take with you when you visit the sitters. I have a brochure at the office that I will send you that might give you some other ideas on what to look for in a sitter. Have you thought about how you will talk with potential sitters about the tube feeding?
Parent:	It's scary to most people who don't know her, but I'm so accustomed to it, I don't even think about it much any more.
Help Giver:	You might spend some time thinking back to how it was for you when you were first learning to give her the tube feedings, and think about how you would teach someone else. You've done so well with the feedings. I'm sure your positive attitude about it will be very convincing for someone who watches her.
Parent:	Yes, her daddy is almost as good at feeding her as I am. I taught him well!

Help Giver:	I've noticed your husband takes a real interest in caring for the baby. Will he be involved in helping find a sitter?
Parent:	I'm sure he would go with me to talk to some people if I asked him. That would be a big help for me because choosing someone will not be an easy decision. He can usually help me see situations a little differently.
Help Giver:	I think that together the two of you will do well with the challenge of finding a sitter. You have several people in mind to contact about names, some ideas on what your expectations are for a baby sitter, and confidence in your ability to teach someone to give the tube feedings. I'll send the brochure I mentioned and call you in a couple of days to see where you are in the process of finding someone to watch the baby.

Help-Giver Roles

Enabling, empowering, supporting, and strengthening families in a way that makes them more competent requires both a shift and expansion in the roles that help givers employ in work with families. We have found it useful to distinguish between a number of different but non-mutually exclusive roles that set the occasion for attainment of the goal of this component of the assessment and intervention model.

Empathetic Listener

Two of the most important roles a help giver can assume are active and reflective listening. In performing these roles, the help giver uses strategies that encourage family members to express and share their concerns about their family and individual family members. As an active listener, one demonstrates interest and concern about what is important to a family and how different members feel or perceive family circumstances (e.g., "You seem very concerned about your child's future. What types of things worry you?"). As a reflective listener, one rephrases what a family says to help clarify exactly what is being said (e.g., "Am I understanding you to say that you have doubts about your child's future, and that this is causing you to feel 'down' and depressed?"). Functioning as a close, trusted source of support and a proactive, empathetic listener are roles that are extremely important if family/help-giver partnerships are to be established. However, it should always be kept in mind that when the complexities of the family's emotional needs are beyond the competencies of the help giver, it is most appropriate to assist the family in accessing professional counseling.

Teacher/Therapist

The role most commonly assumed by help givers working with families of young children is that of teacher or therapist, or teaching the parents to function in these capacities. This is an important role and one that is crucial to the extent that enhancement of child competence will permit him or her to become a more socially adaptive member of the family unit.

As part of home-based interventions in which parents or their care givers are asked to function in an instructional capacity, we find it crucial that, to the extent possible, child-level interventions be incorporated into the daily routines of the family for those efforts to promote rather than interfere with family functioning. In this role, one helps parents find ways of incorporating interventions and therapy into normal daily activities rather than asking families to set aside large amounts of time for teaching. Moreover, in line with our proactive stance toward children and families, assuming the role of teacher or therapist means identifying child and parent strengths and using them as a basis for addressing both child and family needs.

Consultant

The help giver who functions as a consultant provides information and opinions *in response* to requests made by the family or their network members. Families often-times seek advice and information from professionals because they have a need to understand the implications of their concerns and predicaments better. For example, members of a family's informal support network may be reluctant or unwilling to help or assist the family because they lack knowledge and experiences with a certain family situation. In the role of consultant, the help giver provides information that the family requests to make informed decisions and that their social network members can use to be better sources of support to the family.

Resource

One of the most important roles that a help giver can assume is that of a resource to the family. In this capacity, the help giver shares information about different sources of support and resources with the family as possible ways of meeting needs. This is especially true with regard to the types of services and community programs that are available to children and their families. Families are oftentimes not aware of what services exist in the community because of no previous need to access those resources. In a resource capacity, the help giver functions as a natural ''clearinghouse'' of information about community resources, different types of services, and so on.

Enabler

Beyond a familiarity with various services and programs, a family must have the necessary competencies to access those resources. As an enabler, the professional creates opportunities for families to become skilled at obtaining resources and support. In this capacity, the help giver moves beyond simply making families aware of services and programs to helping them become effective and successful in accessing them. The critical element in performing this role is that the family be enabled to take action rather than the help giver acting for the family. For example, rather than the help giver providing transportation for a family to access a resource, the family's ability to access transportation from their social network might be promoted as a basis for getting needs met.

Mobilizer

As a mobilizer, the help giver not only makes the family aware of potential but untapped resources and sources of support and helps them to mobilize support and access resources, but additionally links the family to others (individuals or groups) that can provide new or alternative perspectives on ways to go about meeting needs. As part of the process of helping families identify people in their social networks (relatives, friends, neighbors, employers, clergy, etc.), the help giver and family explore ways in which individuals and groups may be used as a source of aid and assistance. As a mobilizer of support network members, the help giver works to bring together the ''key players'' needed for the family to gain access to resources and support as well as learn from interactions with others.

Mediator

In instances in which families have had many negative encounters with their informal or formal social networks, it is often necessary for the family and the help giver to work directly with different individuals or agencies in a manner that promotes cooperation. One of the purposes of these encounters is to set the occasion for more positive, task-oriented, and mutually reinforcing exchanges between the family and other network members. Mediating interactions and exchanges between the family and other larger systems is a function that should be performed only long enough for the family to begin using its capacity for mobilizing support and accessing resources more effectively.

Advocate

In an advocacy role, the help giver provides families with the necessary knowledge and skills to (1) protect the rights of parents as well as their children, (2) negotiate effectively with policy-makers, and (3) create opportunities to influence establishment of policies on behalf of children and families. This is accomplished in a proactive way, with families, the help giver, policy-makers, and policy-enforcers sharing responsibility for developing and providing services to families.

Guidelines for
Enabling and Empowering Families

Based on an extensive review and synthesis of the help-seeking and help-giving literature, we have developed 12 guidelines that characterize helping relationships that are most likely to enable, empower, and strengthen families as well as promote acquisition of the competencies necessary to meet needs (Dunst & Trivette, 1987). Using these guidelines to implement the first three components of the model should increase the likelihood that families will become enabled and empowered to mobilize their resources to meet needs, which in turn should have positive effects on child, parent, and family functioning. The guidelines, which are stated as a series of operatives in Table 6–8, are described below.

1. *Help is most useful when the help giver is positive and proactive* (Fisher, 1983). Help givers who display a sincere sense of caring, warmth, and encouragement when offering or responding to requests for help are more likely to have health-promoting and competency-producing influences on the help seeker. "When positive help giver motives are attributed (e.g., the help giver is perceived to act out of kindness or generosity), aid is more supportive and results in more favorable reactions" (Fisher, Nadler, & Whitcher-Alagna, 1983, p. 73).

2. *Help is more likely to be favorably received if the help giver offers help rather than waits for it to be requested* (Fisher et al., 1983). Help seeking may be implicit or explicit, and the help giver's sensitivity to verbal and nonverbal messages from the help seeker is key to reading a person's behavior and responding appropriately. Help givers are viewed as more positive by help seekers when they offer help *in response* to client-identified needs (Gross, Wallston, & Piliavin, 1979).

3. *Help is more effective when the help giver allows the locus of decision-making to rest clearly with the help seeker.* This includes decisions about the need or goal, the options for carrying out the interventions, and whether to accept or reject help that is offered (Fisher et al., 1983). To be maximally effective, the choice of refusing help must be explicitly recognized by the help giver, the decision sanctioned, and the opportunity for future exchanges left open as an option for the help seeker to use. Aid that implies few lost freedoms is most likely to elicit a positive response to help giving.

4. *Help is more effective if the aid and assistance provided by the help giver are normative and do not infer deviance or undue variations* (Fisher et al., 1983). Non-normative help is often demeaning and conveys a sense that the family has an inferior status or is incompetent (Hobbs et al., 1984). Help is maximally effective if it does not infer deviance or undue variation from how other members of the family's culture or social network would deal with the same concern or need (Gross & McMullen, 1983).

5. *Help is maximally effective when the aid and assistance provided by the help giver are congruent with the help seeker's appraisal of his or her problem or need* (Fisher, 1983). Perception of problems and needs constitute forces that steer and propel behavior in certain directions (Garbarino, 1982). Positive reactions to help giving are more likely to occur when aid and assistance are appropriate and match the help seeker's appraisal of problems or needs.

6. *Help is most likely to be favorably received when the response costs of seeking and accepting help do not outweigh the benefits* (Gross & McMullen, 1983). The most obvious cost of accepting help is the financial obligation to pay for the resources or services rendered by the help giver. Many response costs are much more subtle, yet greatly influence decisions whether to accept help. Help giving that reduces threats to self-esteem, moderates obligations to pay, protects behavior freedoms (decision-making), and promotes competence and a sense of adequacy is more likely to be seen as personally cost-effective.

7. *Help is more likely to be favorably received if it can be reciprocated and the possibility of "repaying" the help giver is sanctioned and approved but not expected* (Fisher et al., 1983). "Reciprocity is [most] likely to be the preferred mode of reducing indebtedness to the extent that recipients are made aware of this option and they perceive that the opportunity to reciprocate exists" (Greenberg & Westcott, 1983, p. 95). Repaying need not be material in nature and in fact is often informational or emotional. A help giver who provides and accepts aid and assistance makes the exchanges fair and equitable, which in turn bolsters the help seeker's sense that he or she has as much to give as to take.

8. *Help is more likely to be beneficial if the help seeker experiences immediate success in solving a problem or meeting a need* (Nadler & Mayseless, 1983). This is accomplished by using a person's existing strengths to help the person solve small problems, which increases the likelihood of the person experiencing immediate success before tackling more difficult concerns and needs. "If help is given after efforts toward self-esteem enhancement have been successful, it is more likely to precipitate adaptive behaviors (e.g., self-help efforts and subsequent improved performance) than if given before such efforts are attempted" (Nadler & Mayseless, 1983, p. 178).

9. *Help is more effective if the help giver promotes the family's use of natural support networks and neither replaces nor supplants them with professional networks* (Hobbs, 1975; Hobbs et al., 1984). According to Hobbs (1975), help-giving efforts are most likely to be empowering if they strengthen normal socializing agents (relatives, neighbors, the church, etc.) and enhance a sense of community that promotes the competence and well-being of all members in the family's social network.

10. *Help is more likely to promote positive functioning when the help giver conveys a sense of cooperation and joint responsibility (partnership) for meeting needs and solving problems* (Hobbs et al., 1984). Help-giver and help-seeker exchanges that promote participatory decision-making and shared responsibility between the help seeker and help giver set the occasion for the help seeker to feel valued, important, and an "equal."

11. *Help is most likely to be beneficial if the help giver promotes the help seeker's acquisition of effective behaviors that decrease the need for help.* This makes the help seeker more capable and competent (Skinner, 1978). This type of help "enables the recipient to become more self-sustaining and less in need of future help" (Brickman et al., 1983, p. 19), thus promoting independence (Fisher et al., 1983) and problem-solving capabilities (DePaulo et al., 1983). Promoting behaviors that result in the acquisition of competencies that permit greater independence, perhaps more than any other aspect of helping relationships, is the cornerstone of beneficial help-giving and help-seeking exchanges.

12. *Help is more likely to be beneficial if the help seeker perceives improvement and sees him or herself as the responsible agent for producing the change* (Bandura, 1977). It is the "recipient's own belief in [him or herself] as a causal agent that determines whether the gains made will last or disappear" (Brickman et al., 1983, p. 32). Help seekers must therefore perceive improvement, see themselves as no longer in need of help, and see themselves as both responsible for producing the observed changes and for maintaining these changes if help-giving and help-seeking exchanges are to be effective (Bandura, 1977). This sense of intra- and interpersonal control is most likely to be acquired as a function of learning effective, instrumental behavior.

We have increasingly come to realize that it is not simply the provision of support that promotes parent, family, and child functioning, but the manner in which help is provided that has positive or negative consequences (Dunst, 1986a; Dunst & Trivette, in press-c). Our 12 guidelines provide a framework for help givers to evaluate whether they are employing helping behaviors that are likely to be both enabling and empowering.

Table 6-8.
Major Operatives for Enabling and Empowering Families.

- Be both positive and proactive in interactions with families.

- Offer help in response to family-identified needs.

- Permit the family to decide whether to accept or reject help.

- Offer help that is normative.

- Offer help that is congruent with the family's appraisal of its needs.

- Promote acceptance of help by keeping the response costs low.

- Permit help to be reciprocated.

- Promote the family's immediate success in mobilizing resources.

- Promote the use of informal support as the principle way of meeting needs.

- Promote a sense of cooperation and joint responsibility for meeting family needs.

- Promote the family members' acquisition of effective behavior for meeting needs.

- Promote the family members' ability to see themselves as an active agent responsible for behavior change.

Component Outcome

The major outcome of this component of the assessment and intervention model is promoting families' acquisition of competencies that will make them better able to mobilize resources to meet needs. This is accomplished using a "helping style" that enables, empowers, and strengthens families. The guidelines for enabling and empowering families, together with the expanded roles that help givers can assume in working with families, provide a basis for attaining this outcome.

Notes

1. In a previous paper (Trivette et al., 1986), intrafamily and extrafamily resources were considered part of the same assessment and intervention component. We have subsequently separated these resources because each represents a different set of resources that, taken together, increases the likelihood that needs will be met.

2. The major sources of material for these characteristics included *Interviewing: Its Principles and Methods* (Garrett, 1982), *The Skills of Helping* (Carkhuff & Anthony, 1979), and *Shared Decision Making* (Maple, 1977). All three sources are highly recommended for anyone wanting to improve their own abilities to work effectively with families in a manner consistent with the approach described here.

3. These particular qualitative characteristics were chosen because both research evidence and clinical experience have found them to be most important in linking families with resources and needs in a manner that produces positive effects (Dunst & Trivette, in press-d).

7
Case Studies

These case studies illustrate the different ways in which the assessment and intervention process can be implemented in response to family-identified needs. We specifically chose case material that reflected diversity of family backgrounds, living conditions, marital and work status, and other situational conditions that enter into effectively working with families. Some case studies emphasize use of intrafamily resources while others illustrate mobilization of extrafamily sources of support; some case studies focus on family strengths while several stress the ways in which help givers promoted acquisition of parental competencies and skills. *All* of the case studies illustrate the enabling and empowering process and procedures, which can be used to meet quite diversified family needs.

Building Upon Intrafamily Strengths
for Meeting the Needs of a Teenage Mother

by

Sherra Vance

This case study includes several examples of procedures used to identify and meet the needs of young mothers participating in a model-demonstration project for teenage mothers and pregnant teenagers. The material abstracted from the complete case study record illustrates how intrafamily strengths and resources were mobilized to meet needs in a positive, growth-producing manner.

Case Study

"Sandy Johnson," an 18 – year-old single parent of a three-year-old son, David, is pregnant with her second child. She lives with her mother, Judy, her brothers and sister (Rob, 15; Terri, 14; and Tommy, 9), and Billy, her 3 – year-old cousin. Sandy has completed eight years of school and is currently not employed outside the home.

The Johnson family lives in a three-bedroom mobile home under crowded conditions and, because the family is economically poor, they cannot afford better housing. The major source of income for the family consists of monthly Social Security benefits for Sandy's brothers and sister and a Supplemental Security Income allowance for Billy, who is disabled. Although the combined income is usually adequate for meeting basic family needs (food, clothing, and shelter), little money is available to buy any extras that the family desires.

The Johnson's are a close-knit family whose members are very supportive of one other. Judy, Sandy's mother, is a strong-willed woman who is devoted to all family members. During crisis, she manages to pull the family together and promotes a sense of cohesion and a need to "work together." Judy strives to be fair with her children and treats them all with respect. Whenever there are problems between family members or situations that affect the family as a whole, she convenes a family conference to discuss the matter. During these family conferences, everyone has the opportunity to say what is on their minds and share their concerns and feelings.

After finding out that she was pregnant with her second child, Sandy became involved in a model-demonstration project for pregnant teenagers and teenage mothers. Sandy was referred to the project by her mother, who was a volunteer at a preschool program that served as a training site for young mothers participating in the project. This project operates a 20–week work-study program that provides on-the-job training in child care, weekly classes dealing with life management skills, and home visits designed to help participants mobilize their support networks to procure resources to meet individualized needs.

When Sandy entered this project, a number of assessment techniques (self-report scale, group discussion, and interview) were used to obtain information about her concerns, needs, and aspirations. She completed the Resource Scale for Teenage Mothers, participated in a goal-setting session with a group of other pregnant teenagers, and was interviewed to clarify her concerns and interests as well as precisely define her needs and aspirations.

The needs assessment process revealed several major concerns and aspirations. First, Sandy indicated a need to support herself as financially independently as possible, including her son David and the new baby. Second, she indicated a need for additional information about prenatal care so that she could "do the right things" and insure that her second child would have a "good start" in life. Third, she indicated a concern about her three-year-old son's behavior, and that he would "not mind her." Further discussion about this concern revealed a need for instruction about behavior management techniques. Fourth, she felt a need to talk about her feelings about her second pregnancy and what the added demands would mean in terms of "becoming more independent" and "being able to adequately care for her children." Fifth, Sandy aspired to complete high school by obtaining a GED (General Equivalency Diploma), which she saw as a necessity for eventually obtaining a "good job."

The process of identifying potential sources of support and resources for meeting needs began with an assessment of Sandy's personal social network. The findings showed that her network consisted primarily of immediate and extended family, relatives, and a number of human service agencies. Sandy's mother and her brothers were identified as major sources of aid and assistance. She indicated that she and her mother had a close relationship, and Sandy often referred to her mother as her best and most trusted friend. Several extended family members were also identified as potential sources of aid and assistance, including Sandy's grandmother and a number of aunts and uncles. Sandy's grandmother lived next door, and her house often served as a meeting place for family and relatives. Sandy indicated that her grandmother was a tremendous source of emotional support. The agencies that the Johnson family were involved with included an early childhood intervention program, a public health department, and a department of social services.

It is worth noting that Sandy had very few friends her own age in her personal network. She felt this was a result of dropping out of school and living in a fairly isolated part of the county. Although at times she indicated that she wished she had more friends with whom to socialize, this did not seem to be a major concern to her. Sandy also indicated that her oldest child's father, though he occasionally visited her and David, was not a person whom she could depend on. In contrast, the father of the new baby was identified as a major source of support.

As part of identifying Sandy's needs as well as exploring the availability of sources of support for meeting them, a number of individual and family strengths were found to be important intrafamily resources. The ability of individual family members to communicate with one another was a particular quality that produced a tremendous amount of intrafamily emotional support. A second major family strength was the sense of togetherness and cohesion that the family displayed, especially when they needed to "pull together" in times of difficulty. A third family strength was the flexibility and adaptability needed to help one another. Different family members were more than willing to do whatever was necessary when it was in the best interest of individual family members as well as the family as a unit. These particular strengths proved to be major assets for mobilizing resources to meet needs.

Sandy's foremost need was to become financially more independent and self-supporting. Options for financially supporting herself and her children, however, were constrained by several factors. First, Sandy clearly indicated a desire to remain home after the birth of the new baby for at least six months to a year. She felt that this was necessary to provide the child with the attention she believed was needed for the child's development. Second, neither her immediate nor her extended family had enough financial resources to meet their own needs adequately, and consequently could not be looked upon as a potential source of support. Third, even if Sandy wanted to work, the probability of her finding a job was not very good. The county in which she resided had a high unemployment rate, and very few jobs existed for someone without a high school diploma. Fourth, David's father did not work a steady job and consequently could not be depended upon for child-care support. However, the new baby's father did provide some financial support whenever he could.

The process of identifying resources that might be used to meet Sandy's financial needs began with Sandy and the help giver (project staff member) exploring and assessing various options. Given the above constraints, the most logical (and at that time the only) available source of assistance was Aid to Families of Dependent Children (AFDC). Although this is a resource that typically increases the likelihood of dependence rather than independence, the ways in which Sandy went about mobilizing this support source illustrate how even this type of service can be used as an enabling and empowering experience.

After AFDC was identified as an option for meeting her need, Sandy, rather than the help giver, took responsibility for making an appointment to talk to an AFDC case worker at the local social services department. Because Sandy did not drive, the options for getting to the appointment were explored. After a source of transportation was identified, Sandy made arrangements for a family member to transport her to the appointment. She demonstrated quite nicely her ability to mobilize resources in response to an unforeseen obstacle. During the meeting with the case worker, she was told she was not eligible for AFDC as long as she lived with her mother. The case worker suggested she consider public housing, but Sandy rejected this because she would have to live too far away from her family, and she saw the response costs for public housing as far outweighing the benefits. After explaining this to the help giver and other family members, other housing options were explored. Sandy learned that there was a vacant house down the street from her grandmother's, which was once a rental property but had since fallen into disrepair. Sandy nonetheless contacted the landlord, who told her that he wasn't interested in making repairs so that the house could be rented. Sandy suggested a deal to the landlord. She said she would have most of the repair work done to make the house "livable" if the landlord would be willing to agree to a monthly rent that she could afford. When he agreed to this compromise, Sandy convened a family conference to ask if her brothers and mother would be willing to assist with the repairs. They said yes, and the house was finished just before her second child was born. Sandy was especially pleased with "how things worked out" since she was able to remain close by her family, become more independent, and was able to "pull it off" in a way that made her feel good about her own capabilities.

The process of mobilizing resources to meet Sandy's other needs occurred in very much the same way. After further exploration about the types of information Sandy desired about prenatal and infant care and who or what constituted sources of this information, she was able to obtain written materials as well as talk to other parents who shared their knowledge about the topics of interest to her. Her concern about her oldest son "not minding her" was addressed in the work-study program for teenage mothers in which she was participating. Sandy, as part of her on-the-job training experiences, was taught how to use "sit and watch" (a time-out procedure) and other simple behavior management techniques to prevent disruptive and inappropriate social behavior. Sandy's "tutor" discussed the principles behind these procedures and explained how they might be used with David at home. Over the next several weeks, the tutor made a point to ask Sandy "how things were going at home" to discuss what things had improved as well as provide additional information or training. After about six weeks Sandy indicated that David was "better behaved" and that their interactions were much more positive and enjoyable.

The need to talk to someone about her second pregnancy proved to be more involved than initially thought. Originally, Sandy indicated that she was concerned about her ability to care for both David and the new baby adequately, but during group discussions in the life management classes, as well as during home visits made by the help giver, she began to share her concerns about the new baby being a girl who would eventually have a life much like her own (getting pregnant as a teenager, dropping out of school, not being able to have the "little extras," etc.). It proved very important that the help giver function as an empathetic listener as well as reframe Sandy's negative concerns in a more positive way by pointing out how she was "pulling herself out of the trenches" and getting on with becoming more independent and self-sustaining. Sharing her concerns and feelings and getting positive encouragement proved to be a tremendous source of emotional support to Sandy.

It has been six months since her baby, Alice, was born. Sandy still lives in the house she first rented, and her family continues to be a major source of support to her. Alice's father and Sandy are also talking about marriage. He has become a major source of assistance and support to both Sandy and the children. During the last conversation between Sandy and the help giver, she again indicated a desire to obtain her GED. They plan to meet over the next several weeks to begin exploring options and obstacles to completing school, including application procedures, baby sitting arrangements, transportation to and from classes, and so on.

Supporting and Strengthening an Already Competent Family

by
Donald W. Mott

This case example illustrates a number of considerations that are often necessary as part of work with already competent families. The information gathered in work with this family shows how one can build upon and strengthen a family in ways that promote mobilization of intrafamily and extrafamily resources. Implementation of the assessment and intervention process was done primarily within the context of home visits made by the help giver.

Case Study

The "Arnold" family includes Sandi (24 years of age), her 4½-year-old daughter, Judy, from her first marriage, and Steve (30 years of age), who Sandi married two years ago. Both parents are college graduates. Steve owns a building supply company and Sandi works as an office manager. Judy is severely retarded and has a seizure disorder. Although she has command of only a few words, she effectively communicates using sign language and natural gestures. Judy is an affectionate and loving child but is very active, distractable, and has a short attention span.

Our program first became involved with the Arnold family when they moved to our part of the state from a town some 200 miles away. The family first contacted our program when referred for early childhood intervention services by Judy's new pediatrician. The first things that the help giver noticed when she became involved with the family were Sandi and Steve's strengths and unique family functioning style. Their sense of responsibility and purpose, optimism, and positive interpersonal skills were and continue to be some of their strongest qualities. Their ability to communicate effectively with each other as well as with the help giver and other personal network members was a particular strength that made needs identification a rather easy process. The help giver needed only say that she was interested in learning more about the family's concerns and aspirations, and the Arnold's described what they wanted for Judy, as well as themselves.

The Arnolds were most concerned about Judy "reaching her optimal potential." Specifically, they wanted Judy to be able to communicate more effectively, play appropriately with other children, and have the "same opportunities that all young children her age have," despite her sometimes demanding and unmanageable behavior. Further discussion with the family revealed their personal feelings about not being able to "handle and deal with Judy's unusual behavior." They considered themselves quite able individuals, and it frustrated them when they couldn't bring Judy's behavior under control. This threat to their self-confidence was specifically taken into consideration when intervening with the family. Rather than the help giver recommending specific behavioral management techniques, she took the time to find out what the Arnolds were currently doing to handle Judy's behavior to identify what was and was not working. As it turned out, Sandi and Steve were using some fairly effective strategies, and when this was pointed out, with some minor suggestions from the help giver, the parents not only became more able to manage Judy's behavior, but experienced a major boost to their sense of competence as well.

Promoting Judy's ability to communicate more effectively was approached in a rather straightforward manner. First, the ways in which Judy was currently communicating were identified, the functions of the communicative acts specified, and strategies for increasing opportunities for Judy to display these behaviors more frequently during the day implemented. Second, additional methods for promoting communicative capabilities were explored, including the use of sign language to foster Judy's understanding of the relationship between communicative behaviors and their effects on the social environment. Introducing sign language as a means of communication had a significant positive impact on Judy's ability to make her wants and desires known to Sandi and Steve, which in turn decreased some of Judy's undesirable behavior.

The process of identifying and meeting child-level needs in the Arnold family needed to be done in an enabling rather than a usurping manner. On the one hand, both Sandi and Steve were adamant that they be able to manage Judy's undesirable behavior effectively as well as promote and enhance her acquisition of new competencies. Sandi once commented that "unless she was able to get Judy to do what she wanted, it didn't make any difference if someone could get her to talk or play or do anything." On the other hand, the help giver needed to engage in a variety of roles that supported and strengthened the family's desire to be as "competent parents as possible despite Judy's problems." Identifying and building on the capabilities of the family proved to be an absolute necessity in working effectively with the Arnolds.

Beside their concerns about Judy's development, the Arnold's identified a number of needs for themselves that were also addressed as part of the intervention process. One particular need was to talk to other families with children like Judy to get some ideas about how they were coping with their children's behavior. The help giver told the family of a parent-to-parent support project operated by our program. The Arnolds contacted and have met with a number of families, some of which have become close personal friends with Sandi and Steve. Indeed, the Arnolds have done a remarkable job of building an extensive support network of parents whose children have special needs. This network has become a major source of reciprocal emotional support.

A second family-level need identified by the Arnolds was finding someone they could trust to baby sit Judy on evenings that Sandi and Steve wanted to go to a movie or dinner. The process of identifying a child-care provider began with the help giver asking the family to think about people they already knew who might be interested in making some extra money caring for Judy. A number of people, including the daughter of a friend, a teenager who helped watch children at Sunday school, and Sandi's parents, immediately came to mind. The Arnolds, however, were reluctant to ask any of these people to baby sit because they were concerned that they might not be able to "handle Judy" if she became upset or disruptive. The help giver suggested that Sandi and Steve make a checklist of things to do if this occurred and that they instruct a baby sitter in how to care for Judy using the checklist as a training method. Once again it turned out that the Arnolds had all the knowledge and skills required to mobilize resources to meet their needs and that the help giver only enabled the family to do so on its own.

The interpersonal skills that the family possessed were perhaps best reflected in how it dealt with a situation that arose when Sandi's parents began keeping Judy overnight every week or so. Like so many grandparents, they allowed Judy to "get away with things that were not permitted at home." In particular, they would let Judy sleep with them, which undid months of work that Sandi and Steve had put into getting Judy to sleep all night in her own bed. Each time the grandparents allowed Judy to sleep with them Sandi and Steve suffered the consequences for several nights.

When the Arnold's told the help giver of their concern about Judy sleeping with her grandparents, it was quite apparent that Sandi didn't want to "hurt her parents' feelings'' by telling them what they were doing was wrong. At the same time she and Steve could not allow the grandparents to continue to undo everything they had worked so hard to accomplish. The Arnolds asked if the help giver would be willing to talk to Judy's grandparents. The help giver suggested that Sandi and Steve arrange a meeting between themselves, Sandi's parents, and the help giver (who would act as mediator during the meeting) to discuss their concerns. At the meeting, Sandi and Steve told her parents how much they appreciated them taking care of Judy but allowing her to sleep with them made things very difficult at home. The Arnolds approached this difficult encounter in a very positive and proactive manner and were able to get Judy's grandparents to understand their concern. The situation was resolved by the Arnolds using the same checklist they developed for other baby sitters to instruct the grandparents how to get Judy to go to sleep in her own bed.

The examples provided here are just several of the things that the family did to mobilize resources ''on behalf of Judy.'' The roles that the help giver employed in interactions with the Arnolds are best described as enabling and supporting. Both Sandi and Steve continue to do a remarkable job of advocating for the services and resources they need to insure that Judy has everything needed to enable her to have normalized experiences. Now the Arnolds are beginning to tackle the job of preparing the public school for Judy to enter regular kindergarten.

Working With an Already Empowered Family

by
Linda Wortman Lowe and Tina Swanson

The examples taken from the case study described next illustrate the ways in which help givers typically work with already empowered families who ''know exactly what they want.'' The case material also illustrates how parents can balance family and professional commitments that are in the best interests of individual family members and the family as a whole. The interventions that were implemented with the family were done within the context of home visits conducted on a weekly basis.

Case Study

The ''David'' family includes Bill and Mary, 36 and 31 years of age, respectively, their 4 – year-old daughter, Wendy and their 3 – year-old daughter Angie. Bill graduated from college as a business major and Mary graduated from college as a mathematics major. Their youngest daughter, Angie, was diagnosed as having "developmental problems" at about one year of age, although the diagnostic team was unable to identify any specific cause for her developmental delays.

The family recently moved to our part of the state when Bill was promoted to manager of a branch bank. Mary, who is a math professor at a small community college in a nearby town, commutes about 75 miles a day back and forth to her job. The Davids were referred to our program by a staff member from the early childhood intervention program in which the family participated prior to their move. Our involvement with the family began with weekly night-time home visits to identify both the child's and the parents' needs.

The needs of the David family were identified using an interview format that employed "family routines" as the context for getting the family to share concerns and aspirations. Family routines are the day-to-day events and activities that families commit time and energy to either by necessity or desire (meals, putting the children to bed, getting the children to day care, going to church, etc.). The discussion of family routines to elicit concerns has proved a useful way of identifying needs.

A number of concerns and needs emerged from the routines-based interviews. First, throughout the interview, Bill and Mary repeatedly voiced concerns about Angie's current developmental status as well as "what the future would hold for her." Both parents noted their uneasiness about the lack of any concrete reason for her delays in development. Additionally, the Davids shared their feelings about Angie "not making any progress" in her ability to communicate her wants and desires, which in turn seemed to be frustrating to Angie because "no one seemed to be able to understand her."

A second area of concern involved the need for day care since both parents worked full-time outside the home. The Davids had found a neighbor who was willing to watch the children on a temporary basis until they were able to work out more permanent arrangements.

A third area of concern was the need for evening child care since both Mary and Bill were involved in civic and church activities several evenings a week. Additionally, Bill was taking courses one evening a week toward a doctorate in business management, and Mary's work at the community college often required her to be at the college in the evenings and away for several days at a time.

By getting the Davids to share their concerns and aspirations, a number of family strengths emerged as important intrafamily resources. Flexibility and adaptability in "juggling work schedules" in order to take care of the children became readily apparent. Bill was especially accommodating in this respect. Because Mary's work place was nearly 40 miles from their home, responsibility for getting the children to doctor's appointments and picking up the children after work fell upon Bill. A second major strength that became apparent during the interview was

Bill and Mary's ability to make decisions jointly about things that were of concern to them, as well as to agree upon a plan of action. A third major strength was the sense of commitment to the best interests of all family members. On the one hand, Mary and Bill supported one another with respect to their careers and professional aspirations, and on the other hand, it was eminently clear that the parents would do whatever was necessary to meet the needs of their daughters.

Although the Davids had only recently moved into their new home, quite a number of people were named as existing or potential sources of aid and assistance for meeting needs. Bill's parents and several of Mary's relatives, who lived in the town from which they had moved, were named as people they could depend on in times of need. Two of Mary's aunts, for example, were willing to take care of the girls on weekends whenever David and Mary needed to be away. Mary also identified a number of her colleagues as major sources of emotional support, and Bill's closest friend was identified as someone he could talk to about Angie since he was also the father of a child with developmental problems. Members of the church that the Davids attended in their new community were identified as potential sources of support, especially younger members who might be candidates for baby sitting the children at night. Several teenagers who lived in the Davids' neighborhood also might be asked to care for the children. The help giver, who functioned as a resource person for the David family as part of its participation in our program, also provided Bill and Mary with information about day-care and preschool programs they might look into as possible options for daytime child care. Additionally, the resources available to children and their parents from our program were also discussed with the Davids, especially in terms of assessment and support services.

The mobilization of resources for meeting both daytime and evening child-care needs proved to be relatively easy for the David family. After getting information about different preschool options, Mary contacted and visited a number of programs until she was able to find a setting in which both girls could be enrolled and the staff was comfortable with addressing Angie's special needs. Finding baby sitters to watch the children in the evenings was accomplished by talking to church members who shared the names of several teenagers who ''were good with children and could be trusted.''

Bill and Mary's concerns about Angie's current developmental status as well as her future were addressed with a transdisciplinary assessment conducted by our staff with the parents as participating members of the team. The process was begun with a series of home visits to clarify and define precisely what the Davids wanted to accomplish with this assessment. A number of concerns emerged. First, the family wanted to know if any cause for Angie's delay could be identified. Second, the Davids wanted to know more precisely what Angie's current capabilities were and what they could expect in the future (e.g., Would she be able to attend regular classes?). Third, they wanted to know what could be done to facilitate Angie's communication abilities so she would not become frustrated when "telling us what she wants."

The results of the assessment showed that Angie was about one year delayed in development but was functioning at less than a two-year level in the communication area. It was not possible to find any specific factors to account for Angie's delays. The Davids did not find this comforting since it did not meet their need "to know what caused their child's problem," and it was suggested that the parents talk to someone in our parent-to-parent support project whose child was also delayed but with unknown causes.

The results in terms of Angie's capabilities showed that she had a rich repertoire of skills and, although she was delayed, she continued to make progress compared to the findings of assessments conducted by the early intervention program in which Angie previously participated. It was explained to the Davids that based on Angie's "developmental growth patterns" and the progress they could expect as a result of supplemental interventive experiences, their daughter should continue to develop at a slow but steady pace. As it turned out, it was primarily Angie's lack of progress in communication development that overshadowed her skills and capabilities in other developmental domains.

The assessment of Angie's communication skills showed very little use of language but the ability to use naturalistic gestures (extending the arms out to be picked up, pointing, etc.) as a way of interacting with others. A number of options were explored to address Angie's communication needs, including the introduction of sign language, the promotion of communication within the context of daily routines at home, work with the day-care center staff to encourage Angie's use of verbal and nonverbal communication behavior, and "communication therapy" provided by a speech pathologist. The first two options were dismissed by the Davids because the use of sign language was seen as nonnormative and conducting "therapy" themselves was not seen as possible at that time because of their hectic schedule when at home. The second two options were chosen and implemented to address Angie's communication needs.

Now Bill and Mary are quite happy with their ability to juggle their schedules and balance time between careers and family. They are especially pleased with how the children have responded to their "new school" and how well Angie has improved in her ability to communicate. The help giver, who now visits the family every other week, continues to employ the assessment and intervention process for identifying and meeting other needs.

Meeting Family Needs
in a Center-Based Program

by
Lynne Sharpe and R.A. McWilliam

The ability to meet family-level needs during participation in classroom programs requires "on-the-spot" responsiveness to the concerns that families share with classroom staff. In this case example, we illustrate how staff members functioned in different roles (reflective listener, resourcer, enabler, etc.) when parents dropped off and picked up their children from school. Time is specifically set aside for families to share information about their children, ask questions, request information, and so forth in an informal manner. Staff members are highly responsive to concerns and needs that family members express. The ability to meet family needs through their children's involvement in our classroom program has been possible because opportunities are specifically created to do so.

Case Study

The "Russell" family consists of Gail (29 years of age), Tom (33 years of age), their 8 – year-old son Andy, and their 18 – month-old daughter Kelly. Tom, who is a college graduate, is a chemist in a laboratory at a local company. Gail has completed 12 years of school. When the family became involved in our program, the mother was on leave from her job as a sales clerk. The Russell's son Andy had just begun the third grade.

Gail's leave of absence was a result of an incident that happened to their daughter Kelly at about 12 months of age. Just after her first birthday, Kelly contracted a virus that resulted in meningitis. Until that time, she had been a normally developing child. As a result of the illness, Kelly had lost the ability to sit, crawl, eat independently, and "talk." After the illness she was functioning much like a 6 – to 8 – month-old child, and was spending most of her waking hours being entertained by her mother until her father came home from work.

The Russell family became involved in our preschool classroom program when the mother decided she needed to return to work so that the family could pay the bills that had accumulated due to Kelly's unfortunate illness. At the time the mother visited our classroom, she was especially concerned about the type of care Kelly would receive and what the staff would "work on with Kelly" throughout the day. As part of enrolling Kelly in the classroom program, the mother participated in an assessment process that specifically determined the things the family wanted addressed during the school day. The child-level needs that were identified by the mother included drinking independently, communicating using yes-no head nods, playing with toys independently, and sitting and crawling. Each of these needs was translated into a specific set of learning activities that were used to promote Kelly's "re-acquisition" of these skills during her participation in the program.

The process of identifying family-level needs and resources for meeting them occurred in ways that are unique to classroom programs. The major context was the "arrival/departure" area of the classroom. Staff members assigned to receive children as they come into the classroom chat with the parents as they complete a Parent Report Form each morning. The report form includes space for special requests as well as space for parents to indicate needs they have for their children and themselves. This procedure provides a mechanism for active and reflective listening to respond to requests for resources to meet needs.

Shortly after enrolling Kelly in the program and returning to work, Gail began to talk about a particular concern involving evening child-care arrangements. She worried about whether she would be able to find anyone whom she could trust to baby sit Kelly. The staff member told Gail that we had a list of parents of special-needs children who were willing to baby sit youngsters with different handicaps and disabilities. Gail contacted one of the parents and arranged for the woman to watch Kelly and Andy in exchange for Gail watching her children when she needed baby sitting herself.

On another occasion, Gail raised a concern about being able to buy winter clothes for the children because "with all the medical bills, they didn't have enough money to buy any new clothing for the children." The staff member with whom Gail shared this concern told her about an exchange project operated by our agency that would allow her to obtain children's clothing in exchange for Gail providing a service or product. Gail became involved in this project and was able to find suitable clothing for the children in return for doing laundry for another member of the exchange project.

About two months after Gail had returned to work, she began to tell the staff how tiring it was to work full time, do all the household chores, take care of Kelly, and spend time with Andy. It was during this conversation that Gail talked more about the nature of her personal social network, particularly in terms of the roles that her husband, Tom, and relatives played in helping out. Gail said that because Tom's job often required him to work overtime and sometimes on weekends, he couldn't do as much as he would like to help around the house. Gail indicated that both her parents and Tom's parents said they would be willing to watch the children, but she felt this was an imposition. When asked why she felt this way, Gail said she always seemed to be asking them for help and was beginning to feel guilty. When asked how her parents and in-laws felt, she said that they "didn't seem to mind" and really liked to take care of the children. The staff member commented that the children's grandparents might really enjoy watching Kelly and Andy and that they probably did get considerable enjoyment out of taking care of their grandchildren. Gail thought about this for several days and commented that she decided to "take her parents and in-laws up on this offer" to watch the children.

The opportunity for Gail to talk with classroom staff as part of dropping off and picking up Kelly from school has proved to be a simple yet powerful way for staff members to listen and respond to Gail's concerns. Creating such opportunities has been the ingredient that permits family-level needs to be addressed within the context of a classroom program. It has been absolutely essential to sanction and encourage interactive exchanges between staff and parents as a way of identifying needs and mobilizing resources to meet needs. This was accomplished in an enabling manner as the few examples from work with the Russell family illustrate.

Strengthening Maternal Competence as a Way of Enhancing Family Functioning

by
Linda Wilson

The material presented in this case example was taken from work that emphasized supporting a mother's sense of competence as a parent. The case study illustrates some of the steps that were taken to promote acquisition of parental competencies as a particular set of intrapersonal strengths. The work described was done within the context of weekly home visits by the help giver, who created a partnership that permitted mother and staff to pool resources to meet family-identified needs.

Case Study

The "Day" family includes George (39 years of age), Shirley (21 years of age), their 7–month-old daughter Cindy, and David (14 years of age), George's son from a previous marriage. The Days also have a 3–year-old son, Brian, who is in the custody of Shirley's mother in another state. George and Shirley had reluctantly given up custody of their son under pressure from professionals who felt the home was "not adequate for raising a child." The Days are referred to as a "multi-problem" family by local agencies and are under "close watch" in terms of the care of their daughter Cindy.

The Days live in a five-room mobile home located in a mobile-home park. George, who has completed high school, is an assembly worker in a local furniture factory. Shirley, who remains at home to care for Cindy, completed the tenth grade in a special education class. She shared with the help giver that she was labeled mentally retarded in the seventh grade. She also describes herself as having "nerve problems" and has been under the care of a psychiatrist who has prescribed medication for her nerves.

The family was referred to our program by a county homemaker service provider at the local department of social services. During the initial contact with the family, both George and Shirley indicated that their number-one priority was "keeping the family together," especially in light of the fact that they were "forced" into giving up the custody of their son Brian. The Day family has a long history of involvement with professionals from different human service agencies, none of which they speak of in positive terms. Indeed, it was not surprising to find the Days reluctant to allow the help giver from our program to enter their home. Their decision to allow the help giver to visit the family as well as their "acceptance" of subsequent services initially seemed to be based more on their fear of negative consequences than a recognized need or desire for help.

Our program became involved with the Days because of concern about Cindy's development. A number of professionals with whom the family had contact felt Cindy was developing slowly, although the mother described her daughter as just being a "lazy baby." Although the Days were able to repeat the concerns other professionals expressed about Cindy (such as "slow motor development"), neither George or Shirley saw "any problems with Cindy's development."

Establishing rapport and trust was a major emphasis of relationship-building between the family and help giver. It was and continues to be important that the family sees that our program emphasizes supporting and strengthening families in a way that is responsive to family-identified needs. A considerable amount of time was initially spent assuring and reassuring George and Shirley that the help giver would be available to help with things that they and not she felt were important for the family.

Over the course of several home visits, time was devoted to identifying family needs. This was accomplished by having the parents describe things they did with Cindy during daily family routines—dressing the baby, feeding the baby, entertaining Cindy, and so on. It was within the context of describing how Cindy was cared for that Shirley began to express her frustrations about Cindy being a colicky baby who cried a lot and "got on her nerves." When asked how she dealt with Cindy when she became upset, Shirley said she "put the baby in her crib and gave her a bottle to keep her quiet." Further discussion with the family revealed that because Cindy "got on Shirley's nerves," she often became so upset that she could not do the houschold chores.

The discussion with both George and Shirley included numerous negative comments directed toward both self and each other. The help giver attempted to restate and reframe these negative comments in a more positive way to point out the family's strengths and capabilities. Negative comments directed toward one another, for example, were restated in a way that emphasized interest in the well-being of the family (e.g., "George, I can tell it bothers you when Shirley gets upset with Cindy. It's nice to see that you're concerned about your daughter's happiness"). Similarly, Shirley's negative statements about herself were also reframed to point out the "good things she was doing" (e.g., "Shirley, although your sense of frustration is upsetting to you, I can't help but notice how happy Cindy is since you've been playing with her.").

Specific needs were identified by having the Days talk though their daily family routines. These included Cindy's ability to play and entertain herself so that Shirley could get her household chores done, the need for Shirley and George to have time to spend together, Shirley becoming better able to "keep Cindy from crying and keep her happy," and Cindy losing weight (the mother attributed Cindy's lack of crawling and pulling to stand to her being "too fat to get around").

Mobilizing resources to meet these needs was accomplished in a number of ways. First, major emphasis was placed on supporting the things Shirley already did well as a way of building her self-confidence as a mother. This was done by asking her to talk about the times of day that Cindy was the happiest and to think about what she did to keep Cindy this way. Shirley was able to show the help giver the things she did with Cindy to get her to play with different toys, and the help giver suggested ways to use "little tricks" to get Cindy to do other things like rolling over or turning around while on her tummy. Shirley said that at dinner time she had to find a way of keeping Cindy occupied so she could cook and set the table. After some discussion about Shirley's concern, it was discovered that Cindy became fussy and upset about an hour before dinner time because "she gets hungry and doesn't like to wait until her daddy gets home to eat." The help giver suggested that maybe she could feed Cindy dinner earlier, and while Cindy was eating, the mother could have time to fix dinner for the rest of the family.

Identifying a baby sitter for Cindy so that Shirley and George could spend time together proved to be relatively easy. When asked if there were any relatives, friends, or neighbors who might baby sit for Cindy, Shirley mentioned Sharon, George's daughter from a previous marriage, with whom she often socialized. Shirley said she sometimes watched Sharon's two children, who in return would help out in small emergencies as well as help with chores like cleaning the house. When asked if Shirley thought Sharon would be willing to watch Cindy one night a week for two or three hours so she and George could go out, Shirley thought she would and decided to ask her about "exchanging baby-sitting services."

When Shirley brought up the concern about Cindy's weight, the help giver took this as an opportunity to promote more positive interactions with other professionals. When Shirley asked the help giver if she had any information that might change Cindy's diet, she said she was not very knowledgeable in this area but that she remembered Shirley telling her about the public health nurse who had visited the family and had been very helpful to her. Together, the help giver and Shirley made plans for Shirley to make an appointment to visit the nurse, arranged for one of George's children to provide transportation, and planned what Shirley wanted to ask and information she wanted to get from the nurse. Shirley was able to accomplish all of this with some assistance from the help giver, all of which was done in a way that proved positive and helpful.

Just as things seemed to be going better for the family, especially in terms of Shirley's sense of competence as a parent, an unfortunate event occurred. The parents were reported to the department of social services for child neglect, which, of course, the family found devastating. Both Shirley and George shared their sense of anger about this incident, which has "undone" many of the things the help giver and family were able to accomplish. Now the emphasis of our work with the family has shifted to this new concern about expectations of other agencies and the threat of their family being divided.

Promoting Informal Exchange of Support and Resources

by
Lynda Pletcher and Nancy Gordon

The case material described next is taken from experiences with a family participating in a model-demonstration project designed to promote the exchange of resources between project participants in a way that promotes independence in identifying needs as part of both building and mobilizing informal support networks. The portion of the case study presented here illustrates the process employed to accomplish this goal.

Case Study

"Rick and Mary Foster," both 40 years of age, were married after completing the ninth grade. They have spent their entire lives residing in the same rural area. Rick is employed in a local furniture factory as an unskilled laborer, and Mary assumes the traditional role of homemaker. The Fosters, together with their 8 – year-old daughter, Kathy, live in a mobile home in a remote part of the county. Although the family income is quite limited, the Fosters are very competent at managing what money they do have.

Their daughter, Kathy, has been a difficult and demanding child ever since birth. She was an ill and fussy baby and, at three years of age, it became obvious that she was becoming increasingly delayed in attaining most developmental milestones. A developmental assessment at that time found Kathy was functioning between 12 and 24 months in most skill areas. Their pediatrician recommended that the Fosters enroll Kathy in an early childhood intervention program. Now Kathy is in a special education classroom in a local public school.

The family became involved in our program when Mary noticed a poster describing a resource exchange project while attending a meeting at Kathy's school. The poster read "Do you need . . . ?" and then listed things like furniture, clothing, toys, baby sitting, housecleaning, and transportation as products and services that could be obtained as part of participation in an exchange network. The poster went on to say, "It's simple—exchange something you have for something you need."

Mary contacted our program and asked how the services were provided and said that she was particularly interested in obtaining child care. The exchange process was explained to Mary, noting that her need for child care (and other resources) could be met by *exchanging* a product or service with another person who needed something she could provide or do in return. It was explained that resources to be exchanged could be either products a family already had or services they could render. These resources might be clothing, toys, garden produce, craft items, used equipment, household items, or services, such as tutoring, transportation, housecleaning, child care, and yard work.

About a week later, Mary visited our office to talk with a staff member (help giver) to learn more about the exchange network. The purpose of this initial contact was to identify both the family's needs and the resources the family could exchange with other members of the exchange network. This process involved nothing more than the mother going through a list of resources (products and services) and checking which things the family needed and which things the family could provide in return.

Mary indicated that there were four major products and services that could be of benefit to the family. First, she indicated a need for periodic baby sitting and child care so that she and her husband had time to "spend together" and to run errands (e.g., food shopping). Second, she indicated a need for transportation to run errands and "take care of other matters" since she did not drive and her husband's work schedule did not always permit him to "help get things done." Third, Mary indicated a need for someone to repair the steps and porch to their mobile home, which had fallen into disrepair because the family could not afford the materials needed to fix them. Fourth, she indicated a need for clothing for Kathy because they were unable to afford to buy anything new on their current budget.

The process of identifying the resources that the family could exchange for the products and services they desired proved most revealing. At first, Mary was hesitant about participating in the exchange project because she had "nothing to offer to anyone else." However, by going through the "assessment" list of products and services together with the help giver, Mary was amazed at how many things she and her family could do well, and from which others might benefit. The particular things that Mary indicated she could do or provide included housecleaning, window washing, and other household chores; yard work; baby sitting; and companionship. In Mary's case, as well as in so many others, she didn't realize that her family had many resources (intrafamily strengths) of which she could feel proud.

Once resources were identified that both were needed and could be provided, the mother and help giver explored ways in which different people and groups, including members of the exchange network, could be contacted to arrange an exchange. A directory of exchange network members was given to Mary, and the help giver explained how it could be used to locate people who had resources the family needed. The directory is much like the Yellow Pages of the phone book in which different products and services and people willing to exchange them are listed according to areas of residence. At first Mary seemed hesitant about calling someone she didn't know, so the help giver took this as an opportunity to model how an exchange is arranged. The help giver called an exchange network member and explained that she was with a mother who needed child care and was willing to do housework or yard work in return. The network member indicated a need for having some laundry done, and an exchange agreement was made. Mary was to do three loads of laundry (including washing, drying, and ironing the clothes) in exchange for the other member baby sitting her child for six hours the following Saturday.

The process of mediating exchanges for Mary was done on several other occasions to meet her other identified needs. However, as Mary gained confidence in her ability to arrange exchanges independently, she became quite capable of contacting other network members and arranging exchanges on her own without the assistance of project staff.

During the past year, the family has built a functional personal social network and has become quite good at mobilizing resources for meeting needs. The family continues to engage in exchanges with network members, but also arranges exchanges with relatives and friends. Rick's aunt and cousins, for example, have provided child care and transportation to Mary on numerous occasions, and each time Mary reciprocates by doing something in return for them. Mary explained the benefits of exchanging resources to meet needs in the following way: "It's great! It makes us feel good, and we get things we need, too!" The process of building and mobilizing informal support networks as a way of meeting family needs proved very successful in work with Rick and Mary Foster.

Creating Opportunities to Achieve Personal Aspirations

by
Bonnie Walker and Janet Weeldreyer

This case study illustrates the considerations that need to be addressed to help a mother progress toward achieving a personal aspiration. The example is taken from work with a family participating in a model-demonstration project whose major purpose is to enable and empower families to meet their needs through proactive networking between families and agencies.

Case Study

The "Young" family includes John (27 years of age), Mary (26 years of age), and their two children—Becky (7 years of age) and Johnny Junior (3 years of age). John has completed 11 years of school, and works in a mill as a custodian. Mary, who is a high-school graduate, has never worked outside the home except for a part-time job at a local hospital for eight months, which she left when she became pregnant with her first child. Mary and John have lived in the same town since their childhood. Although the Youngs are generally able to "make ends meet" in a variety of ways, they are often unable to meet all of their monthly financial obligations.

The Youngs live in a small two-bedroom home that John inherited from his parents. Mary works hard to keep their home neat and clean. Both the front and back yard are full of beautiful flower beds that were planted by John's mother and that Mary has kept up ever since. The family enjoys living in the neighborhood, and they are close friends with many of the people there.

Becky's preschool years were uneventful, and Mary describes her daughter as a "perfect little girl." She will be entering the second grade this school year. The parents described Johnny Junior as a restless and active child who cannot keep still and "gets into everything around the house." He appears to have no understanding of limits and often goes into the refrigerator and spills food or is found playing in the family car or some other unsafe place. Mary, who remains home with Johnny

Junior during the day, reports that her "nerves are usually worn thin" by the time her husband comes home from work as a result of "trying to keep up with Johnny all day."

The Young family was referred to our program by a pediatric nurse at the local public health department. When Mary brought the children in for their immunization checks, she asked the nurse for help in dealing with Johnny's disruptive and upsetting behavior. The nurse, who had known the family for many years, described our program to the mother, who in turn called and scheduled a time for one of our staff to visit and meet with the family.

During the first home visit, time was spent simply talking with Mary and John and listening to their concerns and aspirations. The family also completed a Family Needs Scale to give additional information about what they thought were their major needs. Not surprisingly, the most important need was finding ways of managing Johnny's behavior. However, further discussion with Mary revealed that it wasn't Johnny's behavior that was her major concern but her inability to have time to get other things done around the house that she found most frustrating. The time demands placed upon Mary "trying to keep up with" Johnny Junior, together with housework, cooking, and so on, proved to be the conditions that were "wearing her down." The need for assistance in caring for Johnny Junior proved to be the major concern that needed to be addressed.

A second project that was identified was an aspiration Mary had for herself. She indicated that she wanted to become a nurse because she felt that a well paying job would permit the family to pay off debts as well as allow it to purchase the "special things" they currently could not afford.

During this initial home visit and subsequent interactions with the family, a variety of family strengths emerged as important sources of intrafamily resources. Flexibility and adaptability between Mary and John Senior were most apparent, perhaps best reflected in the way in which the family obtained a washer and dryer. John spent an entire month working evenings and weekends helping one of his neighbors build a garage, while Mary picked fruits and vegetables from her garden and sold them to a local vendor who operated a roadside stand. The money they made "working extra" was enough to buy the washer and dryer without having to go into debt.

A second major strength was the individual family members' sense of commitment to one another as well as to their community. Despite their poor economic conditions, Mary and John clearly had a sense of pride and accomplishment in the things they were able to do on their own or in cooperation with their neighbors and friends. The Youngs often helped their neighbors in both small and large emergencies and in turn knew they could depend upon the neighbors to do the same. This feeling of reciprocity clearly reflected a sense of commitment, togetherness, and community.

Identifying sources of support for meeting needs and mobilizing intrafamily resources was accomplished using a social network mapping game that permitted identification of existing and potential sources of aid and assistance as well as provided a basis for assessing qualitative dimensions of supportive exchanges. Immediate family (husband, wife, children), Mary's parents, relatives, friends, neighbors, the family doctor, and a nurse at the local health department were identified as the members of the Young's personal social network. Both Mary and John indicated that they were "especially close" to a number of neighbors and that, with few exceptions, most of their relatives could be depended upon in small and large emergencies.

The network mapping process proved especially helpful in addressing Mary's concerns about the time demands placed upon her by the daily care of Johnny Junior. As part of clarifying her concerns and defining needs, several additional considerations surfaced. First, Mary indicated a need for someone to care for Johnny so she could get her household chores done and have the time to pursue her plans to enroll in nursing school. Second, she indicated a need for both immediate "respite" from the demands of caring for Johnny and long-term child-care arrangements.

In exploring options for meeting child-care needs, several sources of assistance were identified. Mary's cousin, who lived nearby, agreed to watch Johnny in return for using Mary's washer and dryer to do her laundry. Mary's mother also agreed to watch Johnny when she needed to enroll in nursing school. Her neighbors, who were aware of Mary's predicament at home and her desire to go back to school, offered to take both Becky and Johnny whenever Mary needed someone to watch the children. Knowing that there were people that she could depend on to watch the children when she needed time to herself or time to get other things done proved reassuring to Mary.

In exploring other options for meeting child-care needs, Mary also indicated that she wanted to look into preschool programs that Johnny could attend. Church-operated preschool classrooms, a mother's-day-out-program, private day-care centers, and a local Head Start program were all identified as possibilities. Mary called several places and visited several others to obtain additional information about hours of operation, costs, and so forth. Given the family's financial situation, the parents decided to enroll Johnny in the local Head Start program, which operated from 9:00 to 2:00 each day. This in turn provided Mary with the time to "think about" schooling for herself.

After Johnny began attending school, the mother and help giver began to discuss what needed to be done for Mary to enroll in nursing school, including application procedures, tuition costs and financial assistance, before- and after-school care for the children, and so on. It was during these conversations that several strengths and concerns became apparent. Mary shared that she had always wanted to become a nurse and that this was a "lifelong goal." However, she wasn't sure how her husband felt about her pursuing this interest since she had never shared this aspiration with him. He had first heard about Mary's ambition to become a nurse during the needs identification process employed with the family by the help giver. Because John didn't say anything to her following the initial meeting, Mary wasn't sure how he really felt about her desire to go back to school. The mother and help giver discussed this concern further, and Mary decided that she would talk to her husband about becoming a nurse.

The next time the help giver saw Mary, she said that she had talked to her husband who shared his concerns but said ''he'd stand by whatever she decided.'' As it turned out, John worried about Mary's health and whether she could be both mother and student. However, he agreed to help around the house, take care of the children so she could study, and ''chip in'' with the chores.

Now Mary is attending a nursing program operated by a local community college. It has been a difficult adjustment for the family, but John, as well as members of the Youngs' personal social network, are all helping out in any way possible to ''make Mary's dream a reality.'' Mary recognizes how hard it has been going to school and taking care of the household, but she is managing quite well.

Responding to the Changing Concerns and Needs of a Family

by
Pat Bell and P.J. Cushing

The material abstracted from the case study record described next illustrates the complexities of responding to the ever-changing needs of a family of a medically fragile child. The case example demonstrates the necessity to make numerous shifts in the focus of intervention efforts as family concerns and needs evolve with every new ''turn of events'' in a child's life. Work with this family was done during weekly home visits by one of our staff members, who functioned in a number of diverse roles over the course of involvement with the family.

Case Study

The ''Williams'' family consists of Douglas and Kathy, 27 and 25 years of age, respectively, and their 4 – year-old daughter, Amy. Both parents are high-school graduates, and Douglas has worked for several years in a service-delivery job that requires him to travel a great deal. Kathy resigned from her job about six months ago, when Amy was diagnosed as having a degenerative disorder that has resulted in progressive neurosis in all areas of the brain.

Amy has been involved in our program since she was one year of age when it was discovered that she had a developmental disorder unrelated to the more recently diagnosed degenerative impairment. Since the time of onset of the latter disorder, there has been a major shift in emphasis in work with the Williams family away from developmental interventions for Amy toward meeting her increasing medical needs and both the emotional and psychological needs of her parents. At the present time, Amy requires a heart monitor and respirator and is under 24 – hour-a-day care.

In the brief time since Amy's degenerative disorder has ''taken its toll,'' a number of specific needs have arisen within the Williams family that have required mobilization of both intrafamily and extrafamily resources. When Kathy and Douglas were first told about the degenerative disorder, they were obviously devastated. Both Kathy and Douglas indicated a need for someone to talk to about the recent turn of events, and a number of members of the Williams's personal social network rallied on behalf of the family. Kathy and Douglas reported that the doctors and nurses who have taken care of Amy, especially her pediatrician, have been of tremendous assistance in helping them understand the causes and implications of Amy's disorder.

Kathy and Douglas have also benefited emotionally from many members of their church, especially their minister. Kathy said that the spiritual support she has received from the minister has been one of the major things that has helped get the family through its recent trials, ''when everything in their lives seemed to be falling apart.'' The family has also found their relatives and friends to be major sources of support: ''somebody to just talk to when things seem like they will only get worse.''

As the 24 – hour-a-day care of Amy began to show its wear on Kathy's physical and emotional health, the help giver commented that ''you look like you could stand a break.'' The mother then shared that she was becoming exhausted and that the need to care for Amy ''all day and all night'' provided little opportunity for her and her husband to spend time alone anymore. Kathy took care of Amy while Douglas was at work, and the father watched Amy when he got home so Kathy could do the housework and run errands; they both often needed to be up most of the night in response to Amy's heart monitor signaling ''trouble.''

After Kathy shared her concerns regarding the increased and sometimes overwhelming demands being placed upon her and Douglas, the help giver asked if she was interested in finding someone to watch Amy a few hours every day or so for her to just rest or do other things that needed to be done. The mother answered with a resounding ''yes,'' and Kathy and the help giver began exploring child-care options. The process began by looking at the Williams's personal social network, including relatives, friends, and neighbors. A number of people were identified as potential sources of assistance, including Douglas's parents and a neighbor who had baby sat Amy in the past. The help giver also told the mother about a specialized child-care project operated by our program that kept a registry of trained child-care providers. The mother began to use these periodically as well as several other sources of baby sitting to have an hour here and there to relax or spend time alone with Douglas.

Just as things seemed to be stabilizing, events "turned for the worse." Amy needed to be hospitalized on several occasions, and the need for 24 – hour-a-day vigilance at home became almost a necessity. There were days and nights that Amy's heart monitor sounded almost every hour. She also had to be placed on a respirator because of increased difficulty with breathing, and her medication regime became more frequent and more complicated.

The worsening of Amy's condition necessitated additional shifts in how the parents responded to Amy's as well as their own needs. The medical bills were piling up, the parents were becoming increasingly psychologically and physically exhausted, and it was becoming more and more difficult for Kathy and Douglas to do things together that they so much enjoyed. Each of these concerns was translated into specific needs in discussions between the help giver and Douglas and Kathy during visits made weekly to the family's home.

Although the father's insurance paid a fair amount of Amy's medical expenses, excess costs were mounting to the point that Kathy and Douglas were not sure how they would ever pay all these bills. Many of the family's relatives and friends were aware of the family's increasing financial obligations related to Amy's medical care and offered to put on a fund raiser to help with some of the bills. The Williams's own families, friends, neighbors, and many members of their church "pulled together" and were able to raise enough money to "take a sizable bite out of Amy's medical bills."

As it became more and more apparent that Amy was going to require specialized nursing care and that friends and relatives could no longer be asked to baby sit Amy, the family and help giver began to explore other options for insuring "the best care possible for Amy." The choices were long-term hospitalization, institutionalization, or in-home nursing care. Kathy and Douglas chose the last option and began exploring means of mobilizing nursing care and ways of paying for this service. The family's pediatrician recommended a home health agency that she had positive feedback about for the care of another child in her practice. Douglas investigated whether his insurance company would pay for in-home nursing care. The help giver told the family about a special fund that was available specifically for in-home care to prevent long-term, out-of-home placement.

Everything seemed to fall into place until additional concerns arose in response to the ways in which selection of nurses was determined by the home health agency and the ways in which the nurses wanted to provide care for Amy. As different nurses showed up nearly every day, the Williamses became increasingly concerned about any one nurse ever becoming knowledgeable enough about Amy's needs to be able to provide "the best quality care possible." When Kathy voiced this concern, the help giver suggested that she make an appointment to talk to a supervisor at the home health agency responsible for assigning nurses to Amy's care to share her concerns and discuss possible solutions. Although Kathy thought this was a good idea, she felt uncomfortable doing this alone and asked if the help giver would attend the meeting if Kathy made an appointment. It was agreed that this was a good strategy, and the help giver and Kathy talked more about what exactly needed to be discussed when they met with the nurse supervisor.

At the meeting with the nurse supervisor, Kathy was able to share her concerns in a way that made the home health professional sensitive and responsive to the Williams's desire for "consistency" in care for Amy. The nurse supervisor expressed her appreciation to the mother for sharing her concerns and assured Kathy that, to the extent possible, she would try to assign the same nurses to the family. The situation has gotten much better, though not perfect, and the family is far more pleased about the nurses that are assigned to Amy's care than they previously were.

When the home health nurses began to care for Amy, a second problem arose. The family's life began to revolve around the wishes and whims of the nurses rather than what Kathy and Douglas thought was in the best interests of the family. Douglas described the situation as "being out of control." The problem was particularly acute on second shift, when Douglas and Kathy were home together. They decided to "tackle this situation first." The following evening, with the help giver (who herself was a nurse) present, Kathy and Douglas shared their concerns with the home health nurse and asked her for suggestions about how they might resolve their "little differences." Kathy and Douglas were particularly good about sharing their feelings concerning the need to be a family and to be able to spend time with Amy any time they wished. The nurse acknowledged that she often became "too involved in just medical considerations" and recognized that Kathy and Douglas had needs as concerned parents that she needed to "keep in mind." This dialogue proved difficult for the Williamses but seemed "to do the trick."

As Kathy and Douglas became more confident about the care Amy was receiving, as well as feeling in better control of their lives, they have begun to spend more time together just relaxing and even occasionally have gone out to visit friends and relatives. Throughout their ordeal, the Williamses have remained a strong, solid family. Their individual and family strengths have been the "glue" that has held the family together, and Kathy and Douglas have been a tremendous source of support to one another. With each new turn of events, they have been able to communicate openly with one another, working together to resolve their differences by "doing whatever needs to be done for Amy." Kathy and Douglas have been remarkable in their ability to deal positively with each new demand placed upon them, and it is clear that their sense of purpose as a family and parents is a guiding force that keeps them going even when things seem to get worse and worse. The Williamses often comment that despite their sorrow and hurt, they "must go on and do the best we can."

Although Kathy and Douglas recognize and accept the fact that it is unlikely that Amy will live another year, they continue to work hard at being a family and do whatever is necessary to help Amy "have the best life possible." In spite of all the ups and downs in their life, they have remained as positive as can be expected. The help giver continues to visit the family each week to work with Kathy and Douglas as they face new demands and ways of dealing with changing needs.

Enhancing the Acquisition of Knowledge and Skills as an Intrafamily Resource

by
Joyce Chase and Janet Weeldreyer

This case study includes material gathered in work with a family participating in a model-demonstration project designed to promote positive transitions between service delivery systems. The case example illustrates how "fear of the unknown" and "failure to recognize one's capabilities" can impede mobilization of resources. The focus of work with the family was on promoting acquisition of knowledge and skills as a set of intrafamily resources that could be used to mobilize extrafamily sources of support.

Case Study

The "Freeman" family includes Jay (32 years of age), Lynne (32 years of age), and their 5-year old son Abe. Jay, who is a high-school graduate, works in a furniture factory as an inspector. Lynne, who has also graduated from high school, has remained at home to care for their son since he was born. The Freemans live in a deteriorated two-bedroom mobile home but are unable to make necessary repairs because of lack of money to purchase needed materials. Both Jay and Lynne have health-related problems, but are generally unable to buy medicine prescribed for their medical conditions.

The family has been involved in an early childhood intervention program ever since Abe was diagnosed as having a genetic disorder. The Freemans were referred to our program at the time Abe was ready to enter public school. The help giver began working with the family specifically in response to the Freemans's request to "get Abe ready to go to kindergarten."

The help giver began working with the parents by trying to get the "big picture" of the family and what they wanted to accomplish for Abe and themselves. A number of techniques were employed to identify the family's needs. The parents were asked to complete a needs assessment scale that the help giver used to get a better idea of their concerns and interests. The Freemans were also interviewed to clarify concerns and more precisely define needs.

The results from the needs assessment process showed that the Freemans had a number of concerns about Abe entering kindergarten. Lynne indicated that she was unaware of how to register Abe; she worried about what school he would attend and what Abe's teacher might be like. Jay was concerned about Abe's safety, since he was quite small for his age. The father worried about Abe getting hurt by the other children. It was also discovered that Lynne worried about the other children laughing and teasing Abe because "he didn't have any nice clothes to wear."

In addition to needs related to Abe's entering kindergarten, a number of family-level concerns were identified. The Freemans noted that they were unhappy about the condition of their home and thought the mobile-home park was becoming an unsafe place to live. Lynne also indicated that once Abe was in school, she wanted to find a part-time job so that the family might be able to afford better housing. Dependable transportation for the family was a third family-level need that emerged during the course of the interview. Lynne described how she needed a way to get to the store to do shopping since she didn't drive and Jay's truck was broken more often than it worked.

After the needs identification portion of the assessment process was completed, the help giver asked the Freemans to consider which needs were most important right now and which ones could wait. Both Jay and Lynne were quick to point out that they were most concerned about Abe entering school. It was at this point that the help giver began to explore more precisely what needed to be accomplished and who or what might be used as resources for meeting needs.

The first concern of the parents was knowing more about what they could expect when Abe entered school. Through further discussion, it was decided that Lynne would talk with a neighbor whose child had begun kindergarten last year to get a first-hand idea about what to expect. The help giver also provided the parents a booklet, *Your Child Entering School*, prepared by staff from the county school system, which included answers to many of the family's questions.

The second concern centered around what things "needed to be taken care of" before Abe could enter school. Lynne and the help giver used the *Your Child Entering School* booklet to make a list of things to be done and then talked about ways to accomplish each of the things on the list. For example, Abe's immunizations needed to be up to date, and it was necessary to make an appointment for a checkup, arrange for someone to transport Lynne and Abe to the health department, and have a doctor complete a health status report that was required by the school system.

A third concern was all the "unknowns" associated with Abe beginning school, like riding the bus, paying for lunches, expectations that might be placed upon Abe, and so on. The help giver suggested that Lynne might want to make an appointment to visit the school and talk to the principal and teachers. Although Lynne thought this would "help relieve her anxieties," she didn't feel comfortable doing this alone and asked if the help giver would be willing to go to the school with her. The help giver said that after Lynne scheduled a time to visit and meet with the school personnel, she would be happy to attend the meeting with her.

A fourth concern raised by the family related to "what Abe would wear to school." The mother proved to be particularly resourceful in dealing with this concern. Lynne, with the assistance of the help giver, was able to rework and mend some of Abe's old clothes to make them look "neat and spiffy." Lynne also became involved in an exchange project operated by our program in which she cleaned a project participant's home in return for used children's clothing.

The process of clarifying other concerns and meeting needs related to Abe's beginning kindergarten occurred in much the same manner. The help giver took the time to "understand the family's concerns" and helped the Freemans translate these concerns into needs for specific resources. Once needs were identified, the family and help giver explored the different possible ways of meeting them by mapping existing and potential sources of aid and assistance to match needs. As options for meeting needs were selected, the Freemans, together with the help giver, developed and actualized plans to accomplish stated goals.

The process of structuring needs identification and resource procurement proved helpful for another reason. During the first several months of work with the Freemans, they often acted as if they didn't consider themselves capable of "taking control of their lives." A major change was noted, however, as progress toward meeting needs occurred. Both parents, but especially Lynne, began to say that "she didn't think she had it in her," referring to her ability to do what needed to be done to get Abe ready for school. Jay, who rarely commented upon the things Lynne did do well, even said that he thought Lynne "did real well" in helping Abe start school.

After Abe was "settled in school and everything was going okay," Lynne, Jay, and the help giver began to address the other needs the family had identified. The first thing the Freemans wanted to do was explore options for Lynne finding a job. This is now the major focus of work with the Freeman family.

8

Family-Level
Intervention Plans

The approach to family-level assessment and intervention described in this book is based upon a converging body of research and clinical evidence regarding the manner in which family-level intervention practices are likely to be both enabling and empowering. The development, implementation, and validation of our family systems model of assessment and intervention come at a fitting and opportune time in light of the passage and enactment of Public Law 99–457 (The Reauthorization of the Education for All Handicapped Children Act). This law includes an early intervention program component that establishes family systems services for handicapped and at-risk infants and toddlers. A major requirement of the early intervention initiative is the Individualized Family Services Plan. The approach to family-level assessment and intervention proposed in this book differs considerably from the manner in which this plan would have us assess and intervene with families. In this section we briefly describe the required content of the Individualized Family Services Plan. We then critique the plan, with emphasis on the faulty logic upon which it is based. Following this critique, we propose a more functional approach to developing family-level intervention plans based on both the material presented elsewhere in this book and other aspects of our work.

The Individualized
Family Service Plan

One of the major requirements of the Early Intervention Program initiative of the recently enacted P.L. 99–457 (Part H) is the Individualized Family Services Plan (IFSP). According to the *Congressional Record* (1986, p. H7895), the IFSP must contain:

1. a statement of the child's present levels of development (cognitive, speech/language, psychosocial, motor, and self-help)
2. a statement of the family's strengths and needs relating to enhancing the child's development
3. a statement of major outcomes expected to be achieved for the child and family and the criteria, procedures, and timelines for determining progress
4. the specific early intervention services necessary to meet the unique needs of the child and family including the method, frequency, and intensity of service
5. the projected dates for the initiation of services and expected duration
6. the name of the case manager who will be responsible for implementation of the plan
7. procedures for transition from early intervention into a preschool program

The IFSP is patterned substantially after the Individualized Education Plan (IEP) required as part of P.L. 94–142. It is our opinion that the IFSP as proposed, is *doomed to failure*. Over the past six years we have been experimenting with the types of formats that are likely to be most useful for developing and implementing family-level intervention plans, including the design proposed as part of P.L. 99–457. We have repeatedly found that the approach to formulating family plans described as part of the IFSP requirements simply does not work very well, sets the occasion for conflict between families and professionals, and often has negative consequences. The IFSP is based upon faulty logic and misguided reasoning that make the utility of the plan, at least as proposed, highly questionable.

One of the presuppositions upon which the IFSP is based is that it is possible (even desirable) to work out long-term intentions, methods, and procedures for meeting family-level needs. This assumption is not only faulty, it is generally unrealistic. We have found time and time again that family needs change so rapidly, sometimes even daily, that by the time long-term plans are formulated and put into writing, the needs have changed and the plan is no longer responsive to what the family considers important enough to devote its time and energy. Our extensive experiences working with families and devising family-level intervention plans have led us to the conclusion that with many if not most families it is very difficult to develop plans that can be so fine tuned that long-range goals, methods, and outcomes can be stated so as to be applicable over extended periods of time. This requirement of the IFSP is simply unworkable and nonfunctional.

A second presupposition of the IFSP involves a requirement that the plan contain a statement of the family's needs relating to enhancing the child's development. This requirement presumes that *all* families identify child-related concerns as needs and goals. On the one hand, this requirement is unfounded because many families often have other needs that take precedence and consume their time and energy. We have found in several studies we have conducted that family-identified child-level needs are inversely related to needs in other areas, and until the latter are adequately addressed, a family will not indicate that they have needs related to enhancing their child's development. On the other hand, this requirement presumes that there should be family-level needs related to the child's development regardless of whether the family views this to be the case. If this is implemented, it will likely encourage a defensive reaction from families, produce negative effects (e.g., increased stress), and potentially have other adverse consequences. Needs statements regarding a family's role in promoting the child's development should be made only to the extent that the family identifies this as a concern or project important enough to devote its time and energy. Otherwise, there will be increased risk of conflict and disagreement between the family and the professional.

A third faulty presupposition of the IFSP is the implicit contention that more is better. The IFSP must include a statement about both the frequency and intensity of services provided to meet needs. This requirement assumes that frequency and intensity are major determinants of successful intervention efforts and ignores the fact that informal treatments can, in many cases, have very powerful effects on family functioning (e.g., providing a parent with written information on the child's handicapping condition, which promotes knowledge of the disability and decreases stress associated with the ''unknown''). This requirement also assumes that needs are static and stable, an assumption that is generally unfounded. It is generally impossible to state with any accuracy the frequency and intensity at which services should be rendered to meet family needs when concerns and priorities change so rapidly. Needs are a relative, changing phenomenon, and interventions to meet needs must change accordingly.

The potentially most damaging aspect of the IFSP has to do with the role the ''case manager'' is expected to play in implementing the plan. According to the *Congressional Record* (1986), the IFSP must contain ''the name of the case manager . . . *who will be responsible for implementation of the plan and coordination with other agencies and persons* [italics added]'' (p. H7895). This requirement states that the case manager and not the family will play an active role in securing resources to meet family needs. This directly threatens a family's ability to become competent and usurps control rather than empowers the family. This particular requirement of the IFSP violates many of the principles of helping relationships that are known to be both enabling and empowering (Dunst & Trivette, 1987). A case manager should not be responsible for implementing the plan. Rather, he or she should assume the roles described earlier so that a family can be enabled and empowered to mobilize resources to meet their needs.

The faulty presuppositions above are but a few examples of the inherent problems and misguided logic of the IFSP. As already noted, we attempted to develop and implement family-level intervention plans from a perspective similar to the IFSP and repeatedly found them to be unresponsive to the changing needs of families. This led us to reconsider how family-level intervention plans should be conceptualized, implemented, and evaluated.

An Alternative Framework for Developing Family Support Plans

As part of our efforts to help families identify their needs and mobilize resources for meeting them, we have found it useful to distinguish between static and fluid family-level intervention plans as a basis for proposing a more flexible and functional approach to developing and implementing family-level interventions. A static plan is one that does not permit, or at least discourages, frequent changes and modifications once goals, methods, and outcomes have been specified. The proposed IFSP is substantially a static plan. (Indeed, a better name for the IFSP is *I*nevitable *F*ailure due to *S*tatic *P*lanning.) In contrast, a fluid plan is one that not only permits but also encourages frequent modifications based on the changes that occur in a family, including the situations and conditions that influence family and child behavior. A fluid plan is one that is responsive to the changing needs of families and thus is both flexible and functional.

Family Support Plan

Based on both our research and clinical experience, while at the same time taking into consideration the intent of P.L. 99–457 (Part H), we propose that the content of a family support plan include the following information:

1. the name of the case coordinator who will function in different capacities to empower families with the knowledge and skills necessary to mobilize resources to meet needs

2. a statement of the child's strengths and current levels of functioning
3. a statement of the family's strengths and qualities that define their unique family functioning style
4. the specific "early intervention" services to be used by the family and the dates the services are started and ended
5. a list of family identified needs, concerns, aspirations, and projects in order of priority
6. a statement of the sources of support and resources that will be mobilized to meet needs
7. a statement of the actions that will be taken to mobilize resources and the role the family will play in actualizing the plan
8. procedures for evaluating the extent to which needs are met

Our method for developing and implementing family-level interventions is relatively simple and straightforward. The assessment and intervention format is divided into two sections and functions as a "working tool" for structuring efforts to mobilize resources for meeting needs and monitor the success of intervention efforts. Section A includes the information listed under items 1, 2, 3, and 4 above. Section B contains the information listed under 5, 6, 7, and 8. Appendix D includes a family support plan form that is both flexible and functional so that the help giver can be continually responsive to family needs.

Because Section B of the family support plan includes the four parts that make the plan both flexible and functional as a working tool, we briefly describe the content of these parts to help the reader see how this information is operationalized in terms of meeting family needs. The four parts include:

1. *A Cumulative Record of Family Projects and Needs.* Family-identified needs and projects are recorded continuously as they are identified and are listed on the family support plan form in order of priority. Needs, goals, projects, and so forth are stated in terms of the outcome that will occur as a result of meeting the need (e.g., child's high chair will be adapted so he can eat dinner with the rest of the family). This component is purposely kept simple so that newly-identified needs can be addressed as they arise.

2. *Sources of Support and Resources for Meeting Needs.* This part includes the particular sources of support that will be mobilized to meet needs and the resources that will be accessed from the support source(s). This includes the people, groups, or agencies that the family has indicated as viable sources of support and the particular aid, assistance, products, services, and so on that will be procured from the support sources (e.g., early intervention program adaptive equipment specialist will design plans to adapt high chair, and child's father will modify chair using these plans).

Table 8-1.
A Rating Scale for Evaluating the Success
of Actions Designed To Meet Individualized Family Needs.

Rating Scale	Criteria
NA	No longer a need, goal, project, etc.
1	Unresolved or worse; unattainable
2	Unchanged; still a need, goal, project, etc.
3	Resolved or attained, but not to the family's satisfaction
4	Unresolved or partially attained, but improved
5	Resolved or attained to the family's satisfaction

3. *Actions and Roles for Mobilizing Resources.* This part includes a statement of the actions that will be taken to mobilize support and the roles family members will play in procuring resources. The actions succinctly state what will be done and who will carry out the plan (e.g., mother will call adaptive equipment specialist to make an appointment to have child fitted so plan can be written; mother and father will take child to scheduled appointment; mother will take child to visit relatives on following Saturday so father can work on adapting the child's high chair).

4. *Evaluation of the Extent to Which the Need Has Been Met or Goal Has Been Achieved.* The proposed procedures for evaluating the effectiveness of the intervention efforts are shown in Table 8 – 1. When the case coordinator has contact with the family, he or she simply records the date of the contact, assesses the extent to which the need is still present, and determines whether the need has been met or the goal has been achieved (e.g., on the first home visit following use of the adapted high chair, mother reports that the child's ability to sit and eat with the family has improved but he can sit only about ten minutes before fussing and becoming upset; two weeks later the mother reports that the family is very pleased and extremely satisfied because the child is able to eat his meals with the family).

This four-part approach for identifying and meeting family needs has been found particularly effective in working with families and represents at least one viable system for developing, implementing, and evaluating family support plans. To be effective in work with families, we must be both flexible and functional in the ways in which we assess needs and intervene to meet them. Family support plans *must* be flexible and functional if we as interventionists are to be continually responsive to ongoing changes in the family system.

Appendix A

Needs-Based Assessment Scales

Family Resource Scale
Support Functions Scale
Resource Scale for Teenage Mothers
Family Needs Scale

A separate packet of the full-size scales for Enabling and
Empowering Families is also available from the publisher.

Family Resource Scale

Carl J. Dunst and Hope E. Leet

The Family Resource Scale (FRS) measures the adequacy of different resources in households with young children (Dunst & Leet, 1987). The scale includes 31 items rated on a five-point scale ranging from *not at all adequate* (1) to *almost always adequate* (5). The scale items are roughly ordered from the most to least basic. The hierarchy is derived from a conceptual framework (Dunst & Leet, 1987) that predicts that inadequacy of resources necessary to meet individually identified needs will negatively affect both personal well-being and parental commitment to carrying out professionally prescribed regimes unrelated to identified needs.

The extent to which the items on the scale form a hierarchy was determined in a study of 28 professionals with extensive experience working with handicapped preschoolers and their families. The scale items were randomly ordered and each subject was asked to rank the items from most to least basic. Correlation analyses were performed between the rankings by the 28 professionals against the order shown on the scale. The mean correlation was $r = .81$ ($SD = 0.09$, $p<.0001$). Twenty-three of the subjects ranked the items on two occasions, two months apart, to establish the test-retest reliability of the hierarchical ordering. The mean correlation for the test-retest rankings was $r = .70$ ($SD = 0.17$, $p<.0001$).

The reliability and validity of the scale were established in a study of 45 mothers of preschool retarded, handicapped, and developmentally at-risk children participating in an early intervention program. Coefficient alpha computed from the average correlation among the items was .92. The split-half (even- vs. odd-numbered item) reliability was .95 corrected for length using the Spearman-Brown formula. The short-term stability of the FRS was determined for all 45 subjects administered the scale on two occasions two to three months apart. The stability coefficient for the total scale scores was $r = .52$ ($p<.001$).

A principal components factor analysis employing varimax rotation was used to discern the factor structure of the scale. The correlation matrix of item scores was factored with unities in the diagonal, and factors with eigenvalues exceeding 1.0 were retained for rotation. A factor loading of 0.40 or greater was used to determine factor membership. The results yielded an eight-factor solution that, taken together, accounted for 75 of the variance. Factor I included items that measure both growth and financial support, including availability of time for personal growth; time for interpersonal relationships; and money for necessities, luxuries, and the future. Factor II included items that assess both health and necessities, including money for food, shelter, utilities, and debts; source of income; job for self or spouse; and health and dental care. Factor III included primarily nutrition and communication items, including adequacy of food, clothing, and transportation. Factor IV included the physical shelter items, including an adequate house or apartment, heat, and indoor plumbing. Factor V was an intrafamily support factor that included time to be with child(ren) and family. Factor VI included items that measure communication and employment, including availability of a telephone, dependable transportation, and source of income. Factor VII was a child-care factor that included child-care arrangements and special equipment for the child. Factor VIII was an independent source of income factor. The factor solutions generally conformed to our expectations that there are separate categories of resources and needs.

The criterion validity of the FRS was determined through correlation analysis predicting personal well-being (Dunst, 1986c) and maternal commitment to carrying out professionally prescribed, child-level interventions (Dunst, 1986d) from the total scale score (sum of the ratings for all the scale items) and several subscale scores of needs. The subscale categories were food and shelter, financial resources, time for family, extrafamily support, child care, specialized child resources, and luxuries. Both the well-being ($r = .57$, $p<.001$) and commitment ($r = .63$, $p<.001$) measures were significantly related to the total scale score. Four of the seven subscale scores were significantly related to well-being ($r_s = .30$ to $.75$, $p<.025$), and all seven subscale scores predicted parental commitment to child-level interventions ($r_s = .37$ to $.54$, $p<.01$). The pattern of significant correlations between resources and well-being is consistent with a burgeoning body of evidence documenting the influences of social support on health outcomes (Cohen & Syme, 1985a). The fact that all eight measures of resources were significantly related to the maternal commitment measure indicates that the influence of adequacy of resources extends beyond well-being to personal belief systems. These results are consistent with evidence from the help-seeking literature that indicates that the extent to which professional prescriptions are seen as relevant for action depends upon the match between personal and professional priorities and needs (DePaulo et al., 1983).

Collectively, the data briefly presented in this report document that the Family Resource Scale is both a reliable and valid instrument for assessing family needs. The reader is referred to Dunst and Leet (1987) for an extensive discussion of the theoretical bases and practical implications of the scale.

Family Resource Scale

Hope E. Leet & Carl J. Dunst

Name _____ Date _____

This scale is designed to assess whether or not you and your family have adequate resources (time, money, energy, and so on) to meet the needs of the family as a whole as well as the needs of individual family members.

For each item, please *circle* the response that best describes how well the need is met on a *consistent* basis in your family (that is, month in and month out).

To what extent are the following resources adequate for your family:	Does Not Apply	Not at All Adequate	Seldom Adequate	Sometimes Adequate	Usually Adequate	Almost Always Adequate
1. Food for 2 meals a day.	NA	1	2	3	4	5
2. House or apartment.	NA	1	2	3	4	5
3. Money to buy necessities.	NA	1	2	3	4	5
4. Enough clothes for your family	NA	1	2	3	4	5
5. Heat for your house or apartment	NA	1	2	3	4	5
6. Indoor plumbing/water.	NA	1	2	3	4	5
7. Money to pay monthly bills	NA	1	2	3	4	5
8. Good job for yourself or spouse/partner.	NA	1	2	3	4	5
9. Medical care for your family.	NA	1	2	3	4	5
10. Public assistance (SSI, AFDC, Medicaid, etc.)	NA	1	2	3	4	5
11. Dependable transportation (own car or provided by others)	NA	1	2	3	4	5
12. Time to get enough sleep/rest	NA	1	2	3	4	5
13. Furniture for your home or apartment.	NA	1	2	3	4	5
14. Time to be by yourself.	NA	1	2	3	4	5
15. Time for family to be together.	NA	1	2	3	4	5
16. Time to be with your child(ren)	NA	1	2	3	4	5
17. Time to be with spouse or partner	NA	1	2	3	4	5
18. Time to be with close friend(s).	NA	1	2	3	4	5
19. Telephone or access to a phone	NA	1	2	3	4	5
20. Baby sitting for your child(ren).	NA	1	2	3	4	5
21. Child care/day care for your child(ren)	NA	1	2	3	4	5
22. Money to buy special equipment/supplies for child(ren).	NA	1	2	3	4	5
23. Dental care for your family	NA	1	2	3	4	5
24. Someone to talk to	NA	1	2	3	4	5
25. Time to socialize	NA	1	2	3	4	5
26. Time to keep in shape and look nice	NA	1	2	3	4	5
27. Toys for your child(ren).	NA	1	2	3	4	5
28. Money to buy things for yourself.	NA	1	2	3	4	5
29. Money for family entertainment	NA	1	2	3	4	5
30. Money to save	NA	1	2	3	4	5
31. Time and money for travel/vacation	NA	1	2	3	4	5

Source: C.J. Dunst, C.M. Trivette, and A.G. Deal (1988). *Enabling and empowering families: Principles and guidelines for practice.* Cambridge, MA: Brookline Books. May be reproduced.

Support Functions Scale

Carl J. Dunst and Carol M. Trivette

The Support Functions Scale measures parents' needs for different types of help and assistance. The scale items were selected from extensive interviews with parents of preschool-aged children. The parents were asked to indicate all of the things that others did that they found helpful and supportive. A taxonomy of needs was generated from their responses, and the resources named most frequently were selected for inclusion on the scale.

An extended and short-form version of the scale include 20 and 12 items, respectively. (The items on the short-form version were based on the factor analysis results of the extended version of the scale.) The scale items are rated on a five-point scale ranging from *never* (1) need this type of support to *quite often* (5) need this type of support.

The reliability and validity of the extended version of the scale were established in a study of 121 parents of preschool retarded, handicapped, and developmentally at-risk children. Coefficient alpha computed from the average correlation among the 20 scale items was .87. The split-half reliability (even- vs. odd-numbered items) was .88 corrected for length using the Spearman-Brown formula. Twenty-five of the parents completed the scale on two occasions, one month apart, to determine short-term test-retest reliability. The average test-retest correlation for the individual items was .91 (SD = .18, $p<.001$). The stability coefficient for the total scale score was .62 ($p<.01$).

A principal components factor analysis employing varimax rotation was used to discern the factor structure of the scale. The correlation matrix of item scores was factored with unities in the diagonal, and factors with eigenvalues exceeding 1.0 were retained for rotation. A factor loading of 0.40 or greater was used to determine factor membership. The results yielded a five-factor solution, which, taken together, accounted for 67 of the variance. Factor I included nearly all the emotional support items (someone to talk to, someone to encourage you, someone to talk to about child-rearing concerns, etc.); Factor II included five child support items (cares for child regularly or in emergencies, interacts with and accepts child, procures services for child); Factor III included the financial support items (lends you money, provides money for basic needs); Factor IV included four instrumental support items (fixes things around the house, does household chores, etc.); and Factor V included two items measuring agency support (obtains services for child).

The factor analysis results indicate that a person's perceived need for support is multidimensional in nature and that there are clearly discernible types of needs categories.

The criterion validity of the scale was examined in terms of covariation between the factor scores, total scale score (sum of the ratings for all 20 items), and a number of parent and family outcome measures, including family well-being (McCubbin, Comeau, & Harkins, 1981), personal well-being (Trivette & Dunst, 1985), and time demands placed upon the respondent (Dunst & Trivette, 1985c). The total scale score proved to be the best predictor of the criterion measures. Both family ($r = .25$, $p<.01$) and personal ($r = .33$, $p<.005$) well-being were significantly related to adequacy of support, whereas lack of support placed more time demands upon the respondent ($r = -.20$, $p<.05$). In contrast, there was considerable specificity with respect to the correlations between the factor scores and the criterion measures. Financial support was the only factor score significantly related to family well-being ($r = .27$, $p<.005$), whereas emotional ($r = .17$, $p<.05$), child-related ($r = .21$, $p<.01$), and instrumental ($r = .29$, $p<.005$) support were significantly related to personal well-being. None of the factor scores were related to the personal time demands measure. The pattern of findings among the criterion and predictor variables generally supported our expectations that adequacy of resources for meeting needs would have stress-buffering and health-promoting influences. These findings are consistent with other evidence that indicates that different components of the social support domain affect health and well-being outcomes (Cohen & Syme, 1985a).

The data accumulated thus far using the Support Functions Scale (Dunst & Trivette, in press-a, in press-b) have shown that an indicated need for support is one of the most powerful moderators of health outcomes in families of preschool-aged children. Thus, the use of the scale for intervention purposes would seem to be strongly indicated.

Support Functions Scale
Carol M. Trivette & Carl J. Dunst

Name _____ Date _____

Listed below are 20 different types of assistance which people sometimes find helpful. This questionnaire asks you to indicate how much you need help in these areas.

Please *circle* the response that best describes your needs. Please answer all the questions.

To what extent do you have or feel a need for any of the following types of help or assistance:	Never	Once in a While	Sometimes	Often	Quite Often
1. Someone to talk to about things that worry you.	1	2	3	4	5
2. Someone to provide money for food, clothes, and other things	1	2	3	4	5
3. Someone to care for your child on a regular basis.	1	2	3	4	5
4. Someone to talk to about problems with raising your child	1	2	3	4	5
5. Someone to help you get services for your child	1	2	3	4	5
6. Someone to encourage you when you are down	1	2	3	4	5
7. Someone to fix things around the house.	1	2	3	4	5
8. Someone to talk to who has had similar experiences.	1	2	3	4	5
9. Someone to do things with your child.	1	2	3	4	5
10. Someone whom you can depend on	1	2	3	4	5
11. Someone to hassle with agencies or businesses when you can't.	1	2	3	4	5
12. Someone to lend you money	1	2	3	4	5
13. Someone who accepts your child regardless of how (s)he acts	1	2	3	4	5
14. Someone to relax or joke with.	1	2	3	4	5
15. Someone to help with household chores	1	2	3	4	5
16. Someone who keeps you going when things seem hard	1	2	3	4	5
17. Someone to care for your child in emergencies or when you must go out.	1	2	3	4	5
18. Someone to talk to you when you need advice	1	2	3	4	5
19. Someone to provide you or your child transportation	1	2	3	4	5
20. Someone who tells you about services for your child or family	1	2	3	4	5

Source: C.J. Dunst, C.M. Trivette, and A.G. Deal (1988). *Enabling and empowering families: Principles and guidelines for practice.* Cambridge, MA: Brookline Books. May be reproduced.

Support Functions Scale
(Short Form)
Carl J. Dunst & Carol M. Trivette

Name _____ Date _____

Listed below are 12 different types of assistance which people sometimes find helpful. This questionnaire asks you to indicate how *much* you need help in these areas.

Please *circle* the response that best describes your needs. Please answer all the questions.

To what extent do you have or feel a need for any of the following types of help or assistance:	Never	Once in a While	Sometimes	Often	Quite Often
1. Someone to talk to about things that worry you 1		2	3	4	5
2. Someone to help take care of your child. 1		2	3	4	5
3. Someone to talk to when you have questions about raising your child 1		2	3	4	5
4. Someone who loans you money when you need it 1		2	3	4	5
5. Someone to encourage or keep you going when things seem hard 1		2	3	4	5
6. Someone who accepts your child regardless of how (s)he acts 1		2	3	4	5
7. Someone to help with household chores 1		2	3	4	5
8. Someone to relax or joke with 1		2	3	4	5
9. Someone to do things with your child. 1		2	3	4	5
10. Someone to provide you or your child transportation 1		2	3	4	5
11. Someone to hassle with agencies or individuals when you can't 1		2	3	4	5
12. Someone who tells you about services for your child or family 1		2	3	4	5

Source: C.J. Dunst, C.M. Trivette, and A.G. Deal (1988). *Enabling and empowering families: Principles and guidelines for practice.* Cambridge, MA: Brookline Books. May be reproduced.

Resource Scale for Teenage Mothers

Carl J.Dunst, Hope E. Leet,
Sherra D. Vance, and Carolyn S. Cooper

The Resource Scale for Teenage Mothers measures the adequacy of different resources in the households of adolescent mothers. The scale includes 31 items rated on a five-point scale ranging from *not at all adequate* (1) to *almost always adequate* (5). The items are roughly ordered from the most to least basic. The scale is a modified version of the Family Resource Scale (Dunst & Leet, 1987).

The reliability and validity of the Family Resource Scale were established in a study of 45 mothers of preschool-aged children (Dunst & Leet, 1987). Coefficient alpha computed among the average correlation of the scale items was the Spearman-Brown formula. The test-retest reliability of the total scale scores was $r = .52$ ($p<.001$) for the scale administered two to three months apart. A factor analysis of the scale yielded an eight-factor solution, indicating that the scale is measuring independent dimensions of resources and needs. The criterion validity of the scale was established with respect to the relationships between the total scale score and both personal well-being ($r = .57$, $p<.001$) and parental commitment to caring for their children ($r = .63$, $p<.001$).

Dunst, Vance and Cooper (1986) examined the utility of the scale in a study of adolescent mothers to identify the determinants of parent and parent-child behavior. The outcome measures included degree of birth-related complications, personal well-being (Dunst, 1986c), and maternal commitment to the care of her child (Dunst, 1986c). The total scale score was used as the predictor measure. The results showed that the total scale scores were significantly correlated with birth-related problems ($r = -.50$, $p<.01$), emotional and physical well-being ($r = .45$, $p<.05$) and the mothers' commitment of time and energy to care of their infants ($r = .54$, $p<.01$). Mothers with more adequate resources were less likely to have birth-related complications, reported better well-being, and were more likely to devote time and energy to the care of their children. These findings support our expectation that adequacy of resources would be related to parent and parent-child outcomes and are consistent with predictions from social systems theory (Bronfenbrenner, 1979) regarding the first- and second-order influences of social support on intrapersonal and interpersonal behavior.

The Resource Scale for Teenage Mothers has been used for intervention purposes as part of a model-demonstration project that emphasizes mediation of support to meet individually identified needs. The scale has proved useful for prompting descriptions of why a respondent indicates a need for certain resources, which in turn helps clarify concerns and translate them into needs statements.

Resource Scale for Teenage Mothers
Carl J. Dunst, Hope E. Leet, Sherra D. Vance, & Carolyn S. Cooper

Name _____ Date _____

This scale is designed to see whether or not you have adequate resources (money, time, energy, etc.) to meet your needs and the needs of your child(ren).

For each item please *circle* the **number** that best describes how well the need is met on a day-to-day basis.

To what extent are the following resources adequate for your family and/or your child(ren):	Does Not Apply	Not at All Adequate	Seldom Adequate	Sometimes Adequate	Usually Adequate	Almost Always Adequate
1. Food for 2 meals a day.	NA	1	2	3	4	5
2. House or apartment.	NA	1	2	3	4	5
3. Money to buy necessities.	NA	1	2	3	4	5
4. Enough clothes for you and your child(ren)	NA	1	2	3	4	5
5. Heat for your house or apartment	NA	1	2	3	4	5
6. Indoor plumbing/water.	NA	1	2	3	4	5
7. Money to pay monthly bills	NA	1	2	3	4	5
8. Medical care for you and your child(ren).	NA	1	2	3	4	5
9. The time and resources (transportation, care, etc.) necessary to complete school	NA	1	2	3	4	5
10. Public assistance (SSI, AFDC, Medicaid, etc.).	NA	1	2	3	4	5
11. Dependable transportation (own car or provided by others)	NA	1	2	3	4	5
12. The time and resources (transportation, child care, etc.) necessary to hold down a job.	NA	1	2	3	4	5
13. Time to get enough sleep/rest	NA	1	2	3	4	5
14. Furniture for your home or apartment.	NA	1	2	3	4	5
15. Time to be by yourself.	NA	1	2	3	4	5
16. Time to be with your child(ren).	NA	1	2	3	4	5
17. Time to be with spouse or boyfriend	NA	1	2	3	4	5
18. Telephone or access to a phone	NA	1	2	3	4	5
19. Knowledge of birth control methods	NA	1	2	3	4	5
20. Baby sitting for your child(ren).	NA	1	2	3	4	5
21. A safe environment to live in	NA	1	2	3	4	5
22. Dental care for you and your child(ren)	NA	1	2	3	4	5
23. Someone to talk to	NA	1	2	3	4	5
24. Time to be with friends.	NA	1	2	3	4	5
25. Knowledge of how to take care of your child(ren)	NA	1	2	3	4	5
26. Time to keep in shape and look nice	NA	1	2	3	4	5
27. Toys for your child(ren).	NA	1	2	3	4	5
28. Money to buy things for yourself.	NA	1	2	3	4	5
29. Money for family entertainment	NA	1	2	3	4	5
30. Money to save	NA	1	2	3	4	5
31. Time and money for travel/vacation	NA	1	2	3	4	5

Source: C.J. Dunst, C.M. Trivette, and A.G. Deal (1988). *Enabling and empowering families: Principles and guidelines for practice.* Cambridge, MA: Brookline Books. May be reproduced.

Family Needs Scale

Carl J. Dunst, Carolyn S. Cooper, Janet C. Weeldreyer,
Kathy D. Snyder, and Joyce H. Chase

The Family Needs Scale measures a family's need for different resources and support. The scale includes 41 items organized into nine categories of needs (financial, food and shelter, vocation, child care, transportation, communication, etc.). Each item is rated on a five-point scale ranging from *almost never* (1) a need to *almost always* (5) a need.

The reliability and validity of the scale were established in a study of 54 parents of preschool- and elementary-aged retarded, handicapped, and developmentally at-risk children. Coefficient alpha computed from the average correlation among the 41 items was .95. The split-half reliability (even- vs. odd-numbered items) was .96 corrected for length using the Spearman-Brown formula.

A principal components factor analysis employing varimax rotation was used to discern the factor structure of the scale. The correlation matrix of item scores was factored with unities in the diagonal, and factors with eigenvalues exceeding 1.0 were retained for rotation. A factor loading of 0.40 or greater was used to determine factor membership. The results yielded a nine-factor solution that, taken together, accounted for 79 of the variance. Factor I included primarily the basic resources items, such as furniture and clothing, child care, health care, transportation, food, utilities, and employment; Factor II included primarily the specialized child-care items, such as specialized dental and medical care, respite care, adapted equipment, and someone to talk to about the respondent's child(ren); Factor III included the personal and family growth items, such as doing things together, educational opportunities, family travel/vacation, and saving money for the future; Factor IV included the financial and medical resources items, such as paying for special child necessities, money for basic necessities, and adequacy of family health care; Factor V included the child education items, such as adequacy of current and future educational placements, child care, and child therapy; Factor VI included the meal preparation items, such as time to cook, help with feeding the child(ren), and adapted equipment; Factor VII included the future child-care items, such as respite care, child care, and the child's future vocation; Factor VIII included the financial budgeting items; and Factor IX included the household support items. The factor analysis results supported our expectations that there are different categories of needs and resources and that families view their needs in a highly personalized manner.

The criterion validity of the scale was examined in terms of covariation between the total scale score (sum of the ratings of the 41 items), the factor scores, and a number of dimensions of parental beliefs (Snyder, Weeldreyer, Dunst, & Cooper, 1986), including well-being, decision-making, and locus of control. The total scale score, reflecting overall adequacy of resources, was significantly related to well-being ($r = .42$, $p<.01$), decision-making ($r = .40$, $p<.01$), and internal locus of control ($r = .28$, $p<.05$). Four of the seven factor scores were significantly related to well-being: basic resources ($r = .52$, $p<.01$), specialized child care ($r = .52$, $p<.01$), financial and medical resources ($r = .48$, $p<.01$), and financial budgeting ($r = .35$, $p<.05$). Four of the seven factor scores were significantly related to decision-making: financial and medical resources ($r = .45$, $p<.01$), future child care ($r = .44$, $p<.01$), financial budgeting ($r = .33$, $p<.05$), and household support ($r = .30$, $p<.05$). Two of the factor scores were significantly related to internal locus of control: specialized child care ($r = .57$, $p<.01$) and financial and medical resources ($r = .43$, $p<.01$). This set of findings is consistent with other evidence documenting the effects of needs and resources on personal well-being and other dimensions of intrapersonal functioning (Cohen & Syme, 1985a; Dunst & Leet, 1987; Dunst & Trivette, in press-a).

The Family Needs Scale was specifically developed for intervention purposes. The scale is used to elicit family-identified needs, and the responses on the scale are used to prompt descriptions of the conditions that influence a respondent's assessment of his or her needs. The discussions that center around the responses on the scale help clarify concerns and help define the precise nature of the family's needs.

Family Needs Scale

Carl J. Dunst, Carolyn S. Cooper, Janet C. Weeldreyer, Kathy D. Snyder, & Joyce H. Chase

Name _____ Date _____

This scale asks you to indicate if you have a need for any type of help or assistance in 41 different areas. Please *circle* the response that best describes how you feel about needing help in those areas.

To what extent do you feel the need for any of the following types of help or assistance:	Not Applicable	Almost Never	Seldom	Sometimes	Often	Almost Always
1. Having money to buy necessities and pay bills.	NA	1	2	3	4	5
2. Budgeting money.	NA	1	2	3	4	5
3. Paying for special needs of my child	NA	1	2	3	4	5
4. Saving money for the future.	NA	1	2	3	4	5
5. Having clean water to drink	NA	1	2	3	4	5
6. Having food for two meals for my family.	NA	1	2	3	4	5
7. Having time to cook healthy meals for my family.	NA	1	2	3	4	5
8. Feeding my child.	NA	1	2	3	4	5
9. Getting a place to live	NA	1	2	3	4	5
10. Having plumbing, lighting, heat	NA	1	2	3	4	5
11. Getting furniture, clothes, toys.	NA	1	2	3	4	5
12. Completing chores, repairs, home improvements.	NA	1	2	3	4	5
13. Adapting my house for my child	NA	1	2	3	4	5
14. Getting a job.	NA	1	2	3	4	5
15. Having a satisfying job.	NA	1	2	3	4	5
16. Planning for future job of my child	NA	1	2	3	4	5
17. Getting where I need to go	NA	1	2	3	4	5
18. Getting in touch with people I need to talk to.	NA	1	2	3	4	5
19. Transporting my child	NA	1	2	3	4	5
20. Having special travel equipment for my child	NA	1	2	3	4	5
21. Finding someone to talk to about my child.	NA	1	2	3	4	5
22. Having someone to talk to	NA	1	2	3	4	5
23. Having medical and dental care for my family.	NA	1	2	3	4	5
24. Having time to take care of myself	NA	1	2	3	4	5
25. Having emergency health care	NA	1	2	3	4	5
26. Finding special dental and medical care for my child	NA	1	2	3	4	5
27. Planning for future health needs	NA	1	2	3	4	5
28. Managing the daily needs of my child at home.	NA	1	2	3	4	5
29. Caring for my child during work hours	NA	1	2	3	4	5
30. Having emergency child care	NA	1	2	3	4	5
31. Getting respite care for my child	NA	1	2	3	4	5
32. Finding care for my child in the future.	NA	1	2	3	4	5
33. Finding a school placement for my child	NA	1	2	3	4	5
34. Getting equipment or therapy for my child.	NA	1	2	3	4	5
35. Having time to take my child to appointments	NA	1	2	3	4	5
36. Exploring future educational options for my child	NA	1	2	3	4	5
37. Expanding my education, skills, and interests	NA	1	2	3	4	5
38. Doing things that I enjoy	NA	1	2	3	4	5
39. Doing things with my family.	NA	1	2	3	4	5
40. Participation in parent groups or clubs	NA	1	2	3	4	5
41. Traveling/vacationing with my child	NA	1	2	3	4	5

Source: C.J. Dunst, C.M. Trivette, and A.G. Deal (1988). *Enabling and empowering families: Principles and guidelines for practice.* Cambridge, MA: Brookline Books. May be reproduced.

Appendix B
Social Support Scales

Family Support Scale
Inventory of Social Support
Personal Network Matrix

A separate packet of the full-size scales for Enabling and
Empowering Families is also available from the publisher.

Family Support Scale

Carl J. Dunst, Carol M. Trivette, and Vicki Jenkins

The Family Support Scale measures the helpfulness of sources of support to families rearing a young child (Dunst et al., 1984). The scale includes 18 items (plus 2 respondent-initiated items) rated on a five-point scale ranging from *not at all helpful* (1) to *extremely helpful* (5). The scale has been used in a number of studies examining the effect of social support on parent health and well-being, family integrity, parental perceptions of child functioning, and styles of parent-child interaction (Dunst, 1985).

The reliability and validity of the scale were examined in a study of 139 parents of preschool retarded, handicapped, and developmentally at-risk children. Coefficient alpha computed from the average correlation among the 18 scale items was .77. The split-half reliability was .75 corrected for length using the Spearman-Brown formula. The test-retest reliability of the scale, taken one month apart, was $r = .75$ ($SD = .17$, $p<.001$) for the average correlation among the 18 scale items and $r = .91$ ($p<.001$) for the total scale scores. The test-retest reliability, taken 18 months apart, was $r = .41$ ($SD = .18$, $p<.05$) for the 18 scale items and $r = .47$ ($p<.01$) for the total scale scores.

A principal components factor analysis employing varimax rotation was used to discern the factor structure of the scale. The correlation matrix of item scores was factored with unities in the diagonal, and factors with eigenvalues exceeding 1.0 were retained for rotation. A factor loading of 0.40 or greater was used to determine factor membership. The results yielded a six-factor solution that, taken together, accounted for 62 of the variance. Factor I included the informal kinship scale items (spouse or partner's friends, own friends, other parents, own children, church); Factor II included the social organization items (social groups/club, parent group, co-workers); Factor III included the formal kinship scale items (relatives, own parents, spouse or partner's relatives); Factor IV included the immediate family items (spouse or partner, spouse or partner's parents); Factor V included the specialized professional services items (early intervention program, professional helpers, school/day care); and Factor VI included the generic professional services items (agencies, family/child's physician).

The criterion validity of the scale has been established in a number of studies with respect to the relationships between the total scale score (sum of the 18 items), subscale scores, and a number of parent, family, and parent-child outcomes (Dunst, 1985). The total scale score was consistently related to a number of parent and family outcomes, including personal well-being (average $r = .28$, $p<.01$), the integrity of the family unit (average $r = .18$, $p<.01$), parent perceptions of child behavior (average $r = .19$, $p<.05$), and opportunities to engage in parent-child play (average $r =$ person's personal social network has been consistently found to be the most potent mediator of personal well-being, and family and parent-child outcomes (average $r = .40$, $p<.001$). Indeed, the positive influences of informal support are so great that aid and assistance from personal network members as a form of intervention are strongly suggested.

Collectively, the data briefly presented in this report document the fact that the Family Support Scale is both a reliable and valid instrument. Its use for intervention purposes is strongly indicated to the extent that a parent's responses are used as a basis for discussion of why certain personal network members might or might not be used as sources of support and resources for meeting needs.

Family Support Scale

Carl J. Dunst, Vicki Jenkins, & Carol M. Trivette

Name _____   Date _____

Listed below are people and groups that oftentimes are helpful to members of a family raising a young child. This questionnaire asks you to indicate how helpful each source is to *your family*.

Please *circle* the response that best describes how helpful the sources have been to your family during the past *3 to 6 months*. If a source of help has not been available to your family during this period of time, circle the NA (Not Available) response.

How helpful has each of the following been to you in terms of raising your child(ren):	Not Available	Not at All Helpful	Sometimes Helpful	Generally Helpful	Very Helpful	Extremely Helpful
1. My parents	NA	1	2	3	4	5
2. My spouse or partner's parents	NA	1	2	3	4	5
3. My relatives/kin	NA	1	2	3	4	5
4. My spouse or partner's relatives/kin	NA	1	2	3	4	5
5. Spouse or partner	NA	1	2	3	4	5
6. My friends	NA	1	2	3	4	5
7. My spouse or partner's friends	NA	1	2	3	4	5
8. My own children	NA	1	2	3	4	5
9. Other parents	NA	1	2	3	4	5
10. Co-workers	NA	1	2	3	4	5
11. Parent groups	NA	1	2	3	4	5
12. Social groups/clubs	NA	1	2	3	4	5
13. Church members/minister	NA	1	2	3	4	5
14. My family or child's physician	NA	1	2	3	4	5
15. Early childhood intervention program	NA	1	2	3	4	5
16. School/day-care center	NA	1	2	3	4	5
17. Professional helpers (social workers, therapists, teachers, etc.)	NA	1	2	3	4	5
18. Professional agencies (public health, social services, mental health, etc.)	NA	1	2	3	4	5
19. _____	NA	1	2	3	4	5
20. _____	NA	1	2	3	4	5

Source: C.J. Dunst, C.M. Trivette, and A.G. Deal (1988). *Enabling and empowering families: Principles and guidelines for practice.* Cambridge, MA: Brookline Books. May be reproduced.

Inventory of Social Support

Carol M. Trivette and Carl J. Dunst

The Inventory of Social Support provides a way of determining the types of help and assistance that are provided to a respondent by different individuals, groups, and agencies that make up a person's personal social network. The respondent is first asked to indicate how often he or she has contact—face to face, in a group, or by telephone—with potential members of the person's social network. This "frequency-of-contact" measure provides a basis for ascertaining with whom and how often the respondent interacts with different individuals or groups. Second, the respondent is asked to indicate whom he or she goes to or receives help from for 12 different types of aid and assistance. (The types of aid and assistance are identical to those on the Support Functions Scale in Appendix A.) Nineteen sources of support—individuals, groups, and agencies—are included on the scale. The sources of support and types of aid and assistance are organized in a matrix format. A completed matrix provides a graphic display of the respondent's personal social network in terms of both *source* and *type* of support.

The scale has been used in a number of studies examining various aspects of a respondent's personal social network (Dunst & Trivette, in press-a). In one study of 120 parents of preschool retarded, handicapped, and developmentally at-risk children, we assessed the extent to which different support sources were used to meet the 12 different needs listed on the scale. The dependent measure was the total number of types of help provided/procured from each support source. A repeated measures analysis of variance yielded significant results, F (18, 2141) = 85.50, $p<.001$, indicating that there were differences in the number of types of help provided by the different support sources. The five most-used sources were spouse or partner ($M = 6.38$, $SD = 4.30$), the respondent's parents ($M = 5.22$, $SD = 4.09$), friends ($M = 4.26$, $SD = 3.97$), the respondent's brothers/sisters ($M = 2.64$, $SD = 3.16$), and the early childhood intervention program in which the respondent's child participated ($M = 2.42$, $SD = 2.26$). The five least-used sources were a private (physical or speech) therapist for the child ($M = 0.32$, $SD = 1.31$), neighbors ($M = 0.80$, $SD = 1.61$), spouse's or partner's brothers or sisters ($M = 0.86$, $SD = 1.90$), child's or family's physician ($M = 0.99$, $SD = 1.13$), and the respondent's own children ($M = 1.12$, $SD = 1.73$).

A principal components factor analysis using varimax rotation was used to determine the extent to which certain support sources tended to provide more or less help and assistance for meeting needs. The analysis produced a five-factor solution that, taken together, accounted for 58 of the variance. Factor I was a formal kinship (I) factor that included spouse or partner's parents, spouse or partner, and spouse or partner's brothers and sisters. Factor II was also a formal kinship (II) factor that included the respondent's parents, the respondent's brothers or sisters, and other relatives. Factor III was an individual source of support factor that included the early childhood intervention program in which the respondent's child participated, private therapist, spouse or partner, and friends. Factor IV was a medical factor that included the child's or family's physician. Factor V was a respondent's children factor. The factor analysis results generally supported our predictions that different types of help and assistance would be provided by different support sources.

The extent to which the factor scores were related to personal (Trivette & Dunst, 1985) and family (McCubbin et al., 1981) well-being were also assessed as part of our study. All but the formal kinship II factor scores were significantly related to personal well-being (r_s = .13 to .29, $p<.05$). Both the formal kinship I (r = .25, $p<.05$) and medical factor (r = .17, $p<.05$) factor scores were significantly related to family well-being. These results are consistent with other findings from our work (Dunst & Trivette, in press-a, in press-b) and that of others (Cohen & Syme, 1985a) regarding the relationship between support and health and well-being outcomes.

The Inventory of Social Support has proved to be an especially useful tool for obtaining a wealth of information about a person's personal social network. The scale has utility for intervention purposes inasmuch as it can help provide insight into who a respondent sees as sources of support and the types of support network members provide.

Inventory of Social Support
Carol M. Trivette & Carl J. Dunst

Name _____ Date _____

This questionnaire asks about people and groups that may provide you help and assistance. The scale is divided into two parts. Please read the instructions that go with each part before completing each section of the questionnaire.

Listed below are different individuals and groups that people often have contact with face to face, in a group, or by telephone. For each source listed, please indicate how often you have been in contact with each person or group during the *past month*. Please indicate any person or group with whom you have had contact not included on the list.

How frequently have you had contact with each of the following during the *past month*:	Not at All	Once or Twice	At Least 10 Times	At least 20 Times	Almost Every-Day
1. Spouse or Partner	1	2	3	4	5
2. My Children	1	2	3	4	5
3. My Parents	1	2	3	4	5
4. Spouse or Partner's Parents	1	2	3	4	5
5. My Sister/Brother	1	2	3	4	5
6. My Spouse or Partner's Sister/Brother	1	2	3	4	5
7. Other Relatives	1	2	3	4	5
8. Friends	1	2	3	4	5
9. Neighbors	1	2	3	4	5
10. Church Members/Minister	1	2	3	4	5
11. Co-workers	1	2	3	4	5
12. Baby Sitter, Day Care, or School	1	2	3	4	5
13. Private Therapist for Child	1	2	3	4	5
14. Child/Family Doctors	1	2	3	4	5
15. Early Childhood Intervention Program	1	2	3	4	5
16. Health Department	1	2	3	4	5
17. Social Service Department	1	2	3	4	5
18. Other Agencies	1	2	3	4	5
19. _____	1	2	3	4	5
20. _____	1	2	3	4	5

Source: C.J. Dunst, C.M. Trivette, and A.G. Deal (1988). *Enabling and empowering families: Principles and guidelines for practice.* Cambridge, MA: Brookline Books. May be reproduced.

		INSTRU

Listed below are 12 different types of help and assistance that people sometimes need and 19 different people and groups who sometimes are asked for help and assistance. For each of the 12 types of help and assistance

Which persons or groups listed to the right provide you help or assistance with each of the following:	Myself	Spouse or Partner	My Children	My Parents	Spouse or Partner's Parents	Sister/ Brother	Spouse or Partner's Sister/ Brother	Other Relatives
1. Who do you go to for help or to talk with?								
2. Who helps take care of your children?								
3. Who do you talk to when you have questions about raising your child?								
4. Who loans you money when you need it?								
5. Who encourages or keeps you going when things get hard?								
6. Who accepts your child regardless of how (s)he behaves or acts?								
7. Who helps you with household chores?								
8. Who do you do things with to have fun, just relax, or joke around?								
9. Who takes the time to do things with your child?								
10. Who takes you and your child places when you need transportation?								
11. Who hassles with agencies and individuals when you feel you can't get what you need or want?								
12. Who helps you learn about services for your child family?								

CTIONS

listed, please indicate which persons or groups you go to when you need these types of help. Indicate who provides you help by checking the appropriate box for the person or group you ask for help.

Friends	Neighbors	Church Members/ Minister	Co- workers	Baby Sitter, Day Care, or School	Private Therapist for Child	Child/ Family Doctors	Early Childhood Intervention Program	Health Dept.	Social Services Dept.	Other Agencies

Personal Network Matrix

Carol M. Trivette and Carl J. Dunst

The Personal Network Matrix provides a way of assessing a number of aspects of needs, resources, and support. The scale is divided into three parts. Part I asks a respondent to indicate how often he or she has contact—face to face, in a group, or by telephone—with different people, groups, and agencies. Part II asks the respondent to (1) list up to ten needs, projects, or aspirations that he or she considers important enough to devote energy to and (2) indicate, for members of his or her personal social network, which people provide or have offered aid or assistance for each of the ten needs, projects, or aspirations. Part III asks the respondent to indicate the extent to which they can depend upon different network members when they are asked for advice, assistance, or any other type of help.

There are two versions of the scale. One version includes preselected persons, groups, and agencies with whom a respondent might have contact. The second version asks the respondent to list the specific persons, groups, and agencies that he or she (a) currently receives help from and (b) might consider as a possible source of aid and assistance.

The Personal Network Matrix was specifically developed as an assessment tool that could be used for intervention purposes. The scale provides a basis of structuring efforts for identifying needs and sources of support and resources for meeting needs. Although the scale can be completed in a self-report format, it is recommended that it be used as part of interviewing a family or family member.

A completed scale provides a graphic display of a respondent's personal social support network in terms of both needs and support sources. It also yields quantitative (frequency of contacts) and qualitative (dependability) information about the respondent's personal network. Collectively, the various bits of information obtained from the scale provide a basis for a help giver and family to explore ways of mobilizing resources for meeting needs.

Personal Network Matrix
(Version 1)
Carol M. Trivette & Carl J. Dunst

Name _____ Date _____

This questionnaire asks about people and groups that may provide you help and assistance. The scale is divided into three parts. Please read the instructions that go with each part before completing each section of the questionnaire.

Listed below are different individuals and groups that people often have contact with face to face, in a group, or by telephone. Please indicate for each source listed how often you have been in contact with each person or group during the *past month*. Please indicate any person or group with whom you have had contact not included on our list.

How frequently have you had contact with each of the following during the *past month*:	Not at All	Once or Twice	At Least 10 Times	At least 20 Times	Almost Every-Day
1. Spouse or Partner.	1	2	3	4	5
2. My Children	1	2	3	4	5
3. My Parents	1	2	3	4	5
4. Spouse or Partner's Parents.	1	2	3	4	5
5. My Sister/Brother.	1	2	3	4	5
6. My Spouse or Partner's Sister/Brother	1	2	3	4	5
7. Other Relatives.	1	2	3	4	5
8. Friends.	1	2	3	4	5
9. Neighbors.	1	2	3	4	5
10. Church Members.	1	2	3	4	5
11. Minister, Priest, or Rabbi.	1	2	3	4	5
12. Co-workers	1	2	3	4	5
13. Baby Sitter.	1	2	3	4	5
14. Day Care or School.	1	2	3	4	5
15. Private Therapist for Child	1	2	3	4	5
16. Child/Family Doctors	1	2	3	4	5
17. Early Childhood Intervention Program	1	2	3	4	5
18. Hospital/Special Clinics.	1	2	3	4	5
19. Health Department.	1	2	3	4	5
20. Social Service Department.	1	2	3	4	5
21. Other Agencies.	1	2	3	4	5
22. _____	1	2	3	4	5
23. _____	1	2	3	4	5

Source: C.J. Dunst, C.M. Trivette, and A.G. Deal (1988). *Enabling and empowering families: Principles and guidelines for practice.* Cambridge, MA: Brookline Books. May be reproduced.

This part of the scale asks you to do two things: (A) Begin by listing up to 10 needs or activities that are of concern to you. We call these things projects because they require our time and energy. Projects include things like finding a job, paying the bills, finishing school, playing with our children, going on vacation,

Which persons or groups listed to the right would you go to for help with any of these projects: Projects	Myself	Spouse or Partner	My Children	My Parents	Spouse or Partner's Parents	Sister/ Brother	Spouse or Partner's Sister/ Brother	Other Relatives
1.								
2.								
3.								
4.								
5.								
6.								
7.								
8.								
9.								
10.								

INSTRUCTIONS

teaching our child how to eat, and so on. (B) After you have listed up to 10 projects, please indicate which persons or groups you go to if you need help with any of the projects. Indicate who would provide you help by checking the appropriate box for the person or group that you would ask.

Friends	Neighbors	Church Members/ Minister	Co-workers	Baby Sitter, Day Care, or School	Private Therapist for Child	Child/ Family Doctors	Early Childhood Intervention Program	Health Dept.	Social Services Dept.	Other Agencies

Whenever a person needs help or assistance, he or she generally can depend upon certain persons or groups more than others. Listed below are different individuals, groups, and agencies that you might ask for help or assistance. For each source listed, please indicate to what extent you could depend upon each person or group if you needed any type of help.

To what extend can you depend on any of the following for help or assistance when you need it:	Not at All	Some-times	Occasionally	Most of the Time	All of the Time
1. Spouse or Partner.	1	2	3	4	5
2. My Children	1	2	3	4	5
3. My Parents	1	2	3	4	5
4. Spouse or Partner's Parents.	1	2	3	4	5
5. My Sister/Brother.	1	2	3	4	5
6. My Spouse or Partner's Sister/Brother	1	2	3	4	5
7. Other Relatives.	1	2	3	4	5
8. Friends.	1	2	3	4	5
9. Neighbors.	1	2	3	4	5
10. Church Members.	1	2	3	4	5
11. Minister, Priest, or Rabbi.	1	2	3	4	5
12. Co-workers	1	2	3	4	5
13. Baby Sitter.	1	2	3	4	5
14. Day Care or School.	1	2	3	4	5
15. Private Therapist for Child	1	2	3	4	5
16. Child/Family Doctors	1	2	3	4	5
17. Early Childhood Intervention Program	1	2	3	4	5
18. Hospital/Special Clinics	1	2	3	4	5
19. Health Department	1	2	3	4	5
20. Social Service Department	1	2	3	4	5
21. Other Agencies.	1	2	3	4	5
22. _____	1	2	3	4	5
23. _____	1	2	3	4	5

Source: C.J. Dunst, C.M. Trivette, and A.G. Deal (1988). *Enabling and empowering families: Principles and guidelines for practice.* Cambridge, MA: Brookline Books. May be reproduced.

Personal Network Matrix
(Version 2)
Carol M. Trivette & Carl J. Dunst

Name _____ Date _____

This questionnaire asks about people and groups that may provide you help and assistance. The scale is divided into three parts. Please read the instructions that go with each part before completing each section of the questionnaire.

Listed below are different individuals and groups that people often have contact with face to face, in a group, or by telephone. Please indicate for each source listed how often you have been in contact with each person or group during the *past month*. Please indicate any person or group with whom you have had contact not included on our list.

How frequently have you had contact with each of the following during the *past month*:	Not at All	Once or Twice	At Least 10 Times	At least 20 Times	Almost Every-Day
1. Spouse or Partner.	1	2	3	4	5
2. My Children	1	2	3	4	5
3. My Parents.	1	2	3	4	5
4. Spouse or Partner's Parents.	1	2	3	4	5
5. My Sister/Brother.	1	2	3	4	5
6. My Spouse or Partner's Sister/Brother	1	2	3	4	5
7. Other Relatives.	1	2	3	4	5
8. Friends	1	2	3	4	5
9. Neighbors.	1	2	3	4	5
10. Church Members.	1	2	3	4	5
11. Minister, Priest, or Rabbi.	1	2	3	4	5
12. Co-workers	1	2	3	4	5
13. Baby Sitter.	1	2	3	4	5
14. Day Care or School	1	2	3	4	5
15. Private Therapist for Child	1	2	3	4	5
16. Child/Family Doctors	1	2	3	4	5
17. Early Childhood Intervention Program	1	2	3	4	5
18. Hospital/Special Clinics	1	2	3	4	5
19. Health Department	1	2	3	4	5
20. Social Service Department	1	2	3	4	5
21. Other Agencies.	1	2	3	4	5
22. _____	1	2	3	4	5
23. _____	1	2	3	4	5

Source: C.J. Dunst, C.M. Trivette, and A.G. Deal (1988). *Enabling and empowering families: Principles and guidelines for practice.* Cambridge, MA: Brookline Books. May be reproduced.

This part of the scale asks you to do two things: (A) Begin by listing up to 10 needs or activities that are of concern to you. We call these things projects because they require our time and energy. Projects include things like finding a job, paying the bills, finishing school, playing with our children, going on vacation, teaching our child how to eat, and so on. (B) Write the first name and last initial of all the people you have

(A) PROJECTS	(B) WHO DO YOU HAVE CONTACT WITH?			
1.				
2.				
3.				
4.				
5.				
6.				
7.				
8.				
9.				
10.				

CTIONS

contact with on a regular basis or who you might go to for help with any of the projects you have listed.
(C) Please indicate who would provide you help with each different project by checking the appropriate box
corresponding to the person's name.

(C) WHO COULD YOU ASK FOR HELP WITH EACH OF THE PROJECTS?

Whenever a person needs help or assistance, he or she generally can depend upon certain persons or groups more than others. Listed below are different individuals, groups, and agencies that you might ask for help or assistance. For each source listed, please indicate to what extent you could depend upon each person or group if you needed any type of help.

To what extend can you depend on any of the following for help or assistance when you need it:	Not at All	Some-times	Occasionally	Most of the Time	All of the Time
1. Spouse or Partner.	1	2	3	4	5
2. My Children	1	2	3	4	5
3. My Parents	1	2	3	4	5
4. Spouse or Partner's Parents.	1	2	3	4	5
5. My Sister/Brother.	1	2	3	4	5
6. My Spouse or Partner's Sister/Brother	1	2	3	4	5
7. Other Relatives.	1	2	3	4	5
8. Friends.	1	2	3	4	5
9. Neighbors.	1	2	3	4	5
10. Church Members.	1	2	3	4	5
11. Minister, Priest, or Rabbi.	1	2	3	4	5
12. Co-workers	1	2	3	4	5
13. Baby Sitter.	1	2	3	4	5
14. Day Care or School	1	2	3	4	5
15. Private Therapist for Child	1	2	3	4	5
16. Child/Family Doctors	1	2	3	4	5
17. Early Childhood Intervention Program	1	2	3	4	5
18. Hospital/Special Clinics	1	2	3	4	5
19. Health Department	1	2	3	4	5
20. Social Service Department	1	2	3	4	5
21. Other Agencies.	1	2	3	4	5
22. _____	1	2	3	4	5
23. _____	1	2	3	4	5

Source: C.J. Dunst, C.M. Trivette, and A.G. Deal (1988). *Enabling and empowering families: Principles and guidelines for practice.* Cambridge, MA: Brookline Books. May be reproduced.

Appendix C
Family Functioning Style Scale

A separate packet of the full-size scales for Enabling and
Empowering Families is also available from the publisher.

Family Functioning Style Scale

Angela G. Deal, Carol M. Trivette, and Carl J. Dunst

The Family Functioning Style Scale is an experimental instrument for measuring two aspects of family strengths: (1) the extent to which a family is characterized by different qualities and (2) the manner in which different combinations of strengths define a family's unique functioning style. The scale items are organized into three categories that are believed to represent distinct (but not independent) aspects of family functioning style: family identify, information sharing, and coping/resource mobilization. The 12 qualities of strong families comprising the content of these categories are based on an extensive review and integration of the family strengths literature (Curran, 1983; Hill, 1971; Lewis et al., 1976; Otto, 1962, 1963, 1975; Satir, 1972; Stinnett, 1979, 1980, 1985; Stinnett & DeFrain, 1985a; Stinnett et al., 1984).

The family-identity category measures five aspects of family strengths: (1) *commitment* toward promoting the well-being and growth of individual family members as well as that of the family unit, (2) *appreciation* for the small and large things that individual family members do well and encouragement to do better, (3) *allocation of time* for family members to do things together (no matter how formal or informal the activity or event), (4) *sense of purpose* that permeates the reasons and basis for going on in both bad and good times, and (5) *congruence* among family members regarding the importance of assigning time and energy to meet needs.

The information-sharing category measures two aspects of family strengths: (1) *communication* among family members in a way that emphasizes positive interactions and (2) *rules and values* that establish expectations about acceptable and desired behavior.

The coping/resource mobilization category measures five aspects of family strengths: (1) *coping strategies* that promote positive functioning in dealing with both normative and nonnormative life events; (2) *problem-solving* abilities employed to meet needs and procure resources; (3) *positivism* in most aspects of living, including the ability to see crises and problems as an opportunity to learn and grow; (4) *flexibility and adaptability* in the roles necessary to procure resources to meet needs; and (5) *balance* between the use of intra- and extrafamily resources for meeting needs.

The scale itself is a self-report measure that can be completed by either an individual family member or the family as a unit. The scale includes 26 statements that the respondent is asked to score in terms of the degree to which each statement is characteristic of his or her family. Each scale item is rated on a five-point scale varying from *not at all like my family* (0) to *almost always like my family* (4).

Several measures of family strengths are obtained from the respondent's scores. First, subscale scores are derived from each of the 12 family strengths areas. (There are two separate coping style subscales.) Second, overall family strengths scores are derived by adding the subscale scores for the family-identity, information sharing, and coping/resource-mobilization categories. Both sets of scores can be plotted on a profile form to discern the family's unique functioning style.

The Family Functioning Style Scale was specifically developed for intervention purposes. It can be used to promote discussions about the ways in which particular qualities function as intrafamily resources for meeting needs. Reliability and validity studies are in progress, and thus empirical support for the value of the scale is yet to come. The scale, nonetheless, does have immediate clinical utility to the extent that it helps identify family strengths and intrafamily resources as well as sets the occasion for promoting mobilization of resources to meet needs.

Family Functioning Style Scale
(Experimental Version)
Angela G. Deal, Carol M. Trivette, & Carl J. Dunst

Family Name _____ Date _____

INSTRUCTIONS

Every family has unique strengths and capabilities, although different families have different ways of using their abilities. This questionnaire asks you to indicate whether or not your family is characterized by 26 different qualities. The questionnaire is divided into three parts. Part 1 below asks you about all members of your immediate family (persons living in your household). Part 2 on the next page asks you to rate the extent to which different statements are true for your family. Part 3 on the last page asks you to write down the things that you think are your family's most important strengths.

Please list all the members of your immediate family and fill in the information requested. When you are finished, turn to the next page.

FAMILY MEMBER	DATE OF BIRTH	AGE	RELATIONSHIP

Source: C.J. Dunst, C.M. Trivette, and A.G. Deal (1988). *Enabling and empowering families: Principles and guidelines for practice.* Cambridge, MA: Brookline Books. May be reproduced.

Listed below are 26 statements about families. Please read each statement and indicate the extent to which it is true for your family. There are not right or wrong answers. Please give your honest opinions and feelings. Remember that no one family will be like *all* the statements given.

To what extent is each of the following statements like your family:	Not At All Like My Family	A Little Like My Family	Sometimes Like My Family	Generally Like My Family	Almost Always Like My Family
1. It is worth making personal sacrifices if it benefits our family	0	1	2	3	4
2. We generally agree about how family members are expected to behave	0	1	2	3	4
3. We believe that something good comes out of the worst situations.	0	1	2	3	4
4. We take pride in even the smallest accomplishments of family members	0	1	2	3	4
5. We are able to share our concerns and feelings in productive ways	0	1	2	3	4
6. No matter how difficult things get, our family sticks together	0	1	2	3	4
7. We generally ask for help from persons outside our family if we cannot do things ourselves	0	1	2	3	4
8. We generally agree about the things that are important to our family.	0	1	2	3	4
9. In our family we are always willing to "pitch in" and help one another	0	1	2	3	4
10. If something beyond our control is constantly upsetting to our family, we find things to do that keep our minds off our worries	0	1	2	3	4
11. No matter what happens in our family, we try to look "at the bright side of things".	0	1	2	3	4
12. Even in our busy schedules, we find time to be together	0	1	2	3	4
13. Everyone in our family understands the rules about acceptable ways to act.	0	1	2	3	4
14. Friends and relatives are always willing to help whenever we have a problem or crisis.	0	1	2	3	4
15. When we have a problem or concern, we are able to decisions about what to do	0	1	2	3	4
16. We enjoy time together even if it is just doing house hold chores	0	1	2	3	4
17. If we have a problem or concern that seems overwhelming, we try to forget it for awhile	0	1	2	3	4
18. Whenever we have disagreements, family members listen to "both side of the story".	0	1	2	3	4
19. In our family, we make time to get things done that we all agree are important	0	1	2	3	4
20. In our family, we can depend upon the support of one another whenever something goes wrong	0	1	2	3	4
21. We generally talk about the different ways we deal with problems or concerns	0	1	2	3	4
22. In our family, our relationships will outlast our material possessions	0	1	2	3	4
23. Decisions like moving or changing jobs are based on what is best for all family members.	0	1	2	3	4
24. We can depend upon one another to help out when something unexpected comes up	0	1	2	3	4
25. In our family, we try not to take one another for granted	0	1	2	3	4
26. We try to solve our problems first before asking others to help	0	1	2	3	4

Please write down all things that you consider to be the major strengths of your family. Don't overlook the little things that occur everyday which we often take for granted (e.g., sharing the responsibility of getting your child fed and to school).

Family Functioning Style Scale
(Experimental Version)
Angela G. Deal, Carol M. Trivette, & Carl J. Dunst

Scoring and Profiling Form

Respondent _____ Date _____ Recorder _____

DIRECTIONS

The scoring profiling process is designed to facilitate accurate summation of responses on The Family Functioning Style Scale. The scoring sheet includes spaces for individual item scores, subscale scores, and category scores. The recorder should first enter the item score on the scoring sheet and then sum them to obtain the subscale score. The subscale scores for these separate categories of family strengths are them summed to obtain category scores. The subscale and category scores from the scoring sheets are transferred to the profile form by simply circling the number corresponding to the scores. The circled numbers are then corrected by pencil or pen to depict a family's profile of strengths.

Source: C.J. Dunst, C.M. Trivette, and A.G. Deal (1988). *Enabling and empowering families: Principles and guidelines for practice.* Cambridge, MA: Brookline Books. May be reproduced.

SCORING SHEET

Item	Commitment	Appreciation	Time	Sense of Purpose	Congruence	Communication	Role Expectations	Coping (I)	Coping (II)	Problem Solving	Positivism	Flexibility	Balance	CATEGORY SCORE
1	☐													
2							☐							
3											☐			
4		☐												
5						☐								
6				☐										
7													☐	
8					☐									
9												☐		
10								☐						
11											☐			
12			☐											
13						☐								
14									☐					
15										☐				
16			☐											
17								☐						
18						☐								
19					☐									
20									☐					
21										☐				
22				☐										
23	☐													
24												☐		
25		☐												
26													☐	
Subscale Score														

Family Identity   ☐ + ☐ + ☐ + ☐ = ... ☐

Information Sharing   ☐ + ☐ = ... ☐

Coping/ Resource Mobilization   ☐ + ☐ + ☐ + ☐ + ☐ + ☐ = ☐

FAMILY FUNCTIONING STYLE SCALE

PROFILE FORM

Family Identity	Commitment..........	0	1	2	3	4	5	6	7	8
	Appreciation...........	0	1	2	3	4	5	6	7	8
	Time....................	0	1	2	3	4	5	6	7	8
	Sense of Purpose.....	0	1	2	3	4	5	6	7	8
	Congruence...........	0	1	2	3	4	5	6	7	8
Information Sharing	Communication.......	0	1	2	3	4	5	6	7	8
	Role Expectations.....	0	1	2	3	4	5	6	7	8
Coping/Resource Mobilization	Coping I................	0	1	2	3	4	5	6	7	8
	Coping II..............	0	1	2	3	4	5	6	7	8
	Problem Solving.......	0	1	2	3	4	5	6	7	8
	Positivism.............	0	1	2	3	4	5	6	7	8
	Flexibility.............	0	1	2	3	4	5	6	7	8
	Balance...............	0	1	2	3	4	5	6	7	8

Family Identity	0 ....10..........20 ....30 40
Information Sharing	0 . . . 4 . . . 8 . . . 12 . . . 16
Coping/Resource Mobilization	0 ....12...........24 ....36 48

Appendix D
Family Support Plan

A separate packet of the full-size scales for Enabling and
Empowering Families is also available from the publisher.

Family Support Plan

Carl J. Dunst, Carol M. Trivette, and Angela G. Deal

The system that we have developed for writing and implementing the Family Support Plan is both flexible and functional. The format not only permits but also encourages frequent modifications in response to the changing needs, interests, and aspirations of families and individual family members. Our Family Support Plan is divided into two major sections. Section I provides space for describing a number of aspects of family relationships and child and family behavior. Section II provides space for recording information necessary for designing, implementing, and evaluating plans for mobilizing resources for meeting needs.

Section I

Section I has five parts. Part 1 is for recording the family's name and the name of the case coordinator (help giver) who will function in a number of capacities to enable and empower families. Part 2 provides space for recording the names of immediate family members, their dates of birth and ages, and their relationship to the target child. Immediate family includes all person's living in the family's household on a regular or permanent basis. Part 3 is for recording the child's current levels of functioning according to developmental domain, age level, and age range, and for describing the child's major strengths. Part 4 is for recording family strengths according to the three major categories of family functioning style. Part 5 is for recording both the particular informal and formal services (types of family/child involvement) that are to be used by the family and the dates these services are started and ended. Family and child involvement might include such varied things as parent support groups, the child's enrollment in a preschool classroom, physical or speech therapy for the child, parent participation in a training program, or any other type of involvement *specifically* chosen to meet one or more family identified needs.

Section II

Section II also has five parts. Part 1 is for recording the family's name, the name of the case coordinator, and the page number of the cumulative record of the Family Support Plan. Part 2 is for recording each family need and project as it is identified as well as for recording the dates on which the needs and projects were identified. Needs should be stated in an "in order to" format so that the purpose of procuring a resource is as clear as possible. For example, a mother's need for information about her child's handicapping condition might be stated as follows: "Mother will obtain written materials about X syndrome in order to become more knowledgeable about Johnny's condition." Part 3 is for recording the specific resources that will be procured to meet the family's need and the source of support for the resources. This need not include anything more than a brief statement or list of support sources and resources that will be mobilized. Part 4 is for a brief description of what actions will be taken to mobilize the resources necessary for meeting needs. The actions should be stated succinctly in terms of what will be done and who will be responsible for accomplishing and carrying out the actions. Part 5 is for evaluating the extent to which needs are met as a result of actions designed to mobilize resources.

The case coordinator should add Section II pages as additional family needs are addressed. The case coordinator need only number the additional Section II pages sequentially to have a cumulative record of work with the family.

Additional Features

The recommended rating scale for evaluating efforts to meet family-identified needs is included on the last page of the Family Support Plan. When the case coordinator has any type of contact with the family, he or she simply records the date of contact, assesses the extent to which the need is still present, and determines whether the need has been met or the goal or project has been achieved. The last page of the Family Support Plan also includes space for recording notes or making comments about those aspects of working with the family that are not reflected on any other part of the written document.

Collectively, the format of our Family Support Plan provides a simple yet efficient system for identifying and meeting family needs as well as evaluating the efficacy of efforts to mobilize resources. The simplicity of our plan is by design so that case coordinators spend most of their time employing help-giving behavior that enables and empowers families rather than "pushing paper" that no one will ever read or use.

Family Support Plan

Family Name _____ Case Coordinator _____

FAMILY MEMBER	DATE OF BIRTH	AGE	RELATIONSHIP

CHILD'S FUNCTIONING LEVEL			CHILD'S STRENGTHS
Domain	Age Level	Age Range	

FAMILY STRENGTHS		
Family Identity	Information Sharing	Coping/Resource Mobilization

FAMILY/CHILD INVOLVEMENT	DATES	
	Started	Ended

Source: C.J. Dunst, C.M. Trivette, and A.G. Deal (1988). *Enabling and empowering families: Principles and guidelines for practice.* Cambridge, MA: Brookline Books. May be reproduced.

Family _____ Case Coordinator

DATE	NEED/PROJECT	SOURCE OF SUPPORT/RESOURCE

Page Number

ACTION	EVALUATION DATE									

EVALUATION RATING SCALE	
Ratings	Criteria
NA	No Longer a Need, Goal, Aspiration, or Project
1	Unresolved or Worse; Unattainable
2	Unchanged; Still a Need, Goal, Aspiration, or Project
3	Resolved or Attained; But Not to the Family's Satisfaction
4	Unresolved or Partially Attained, But Improved
5	Resolved or Attained to the Family's Satisfaction

DATE	NOTES/COMMENTS

Appendix E
Profile of Family Needs
and Social Support

Profile of Family Needs and Social Support
Carol M. Trivette, Carl J. Dunst, & Angela G. Deal

Recording Form

Family Name _____   Interviewer _____

INSTRUCTIONS
The Profile of Family Needs and Social Support provides a way of recording (a) the needs, projects and aspirations that a family considers important enough to devote time and energy and (b) the persons, groups, and agencies that constitute sources of support and resources for meeting needs. Space is provided for listing a family's needs and projects down the left-hand column and listing both existing and potential support sources across the top portion of the recording form. The middle part of the matrix provides space for recording particular resources that are to be procured from the different support sources for meeting family-identified needs.

FAMILY MEMBER	DATE OF BIRTH	AGE	RELATIONSHIP

NEED/PROJECT		

SOURCE OF SUPPORT AND RESOURCES

NOTES

Appendix F
Family Strengths Profile

A separate packet of the full-size scales for Enabling and
Empowering Families is also available from the publisher.

Family Strengths Profile
Carol M. Trivette, Carl J. Dunst, & Angela G. Deal

Recording Form

Family Name _____ Interviewer _____

INSTRUCTIONS
The Family Strengths Profile provides a way of recording family behaviors and noting the particular strengths and resources that the behaviors reflect. Space is provided down the left-hand column of the recording form for listing behavior exemplars. For each behavior listed, the interviewer simply checks which particular qualities are characterized by the family behavior. (Space is also provided to record other qualities not listed.) The interviewer also notes whether the behavior is viewed as a way of mobilizing intrafamily or extrafamily resources, or both. A completed matrix provides a graphic display of a family's unique functioning style.

FAMILY MEMBER	DATE OF BIRTH	AGE	RELATIONSHIP

Source: C.J. Dunst, C.M. Trivette, and A.G. Deal (1988). *Enabling and empowering families: Principles and guidelines for practice.* Cambridge, MA: Brookline Books. May be reproduced.

FAMILY BEHAVIOR	Commitment	Appreciation	Time	Sense of Purpose	Congruence	Communication

FAMILY STRENGTHS									TYPE OF RESOURCE	
Role Expectations	Coping Strategies	Problem Solving	Positivism	Flexibility	Balance				Intrafamily	Extrafamily

NOTES

References

Affleck, G., Tennen, H., Allen, D.A., & Gershman, K. (1986). Perceived social support and maternal adaptation during the transition from hospital to home care of high-risk infants. *Infant Mental Health Journal*, *7*, 6–18.

Bandura, A. (1975). The ethics and social purposes of behavior modification. In C.M. Franks & G.T. Wilson (Eds.), *Annual review of behavior therapy theory and practice* (pp. 13–22). New York: Brunner/Mazel.

Bandura, A. (1977). Self-efficacy: Toward a unifying theory of behavioral change. *Psychological Review*, *84*, 191–215.

Bandura, A. (1982). Self-efficacy mechanism in human agency. *American Psychologist*, *37*, 122–147.

Barrera, M. (1986). Distinctions between social concepts, measures, and models. *American Journal of Community Psychology*, *14*, 413–445.

Brandtstadter, J. (1980). Relationships between life-span developmental theory, research, and intervention: A revision of some stereotypes. In R.R. Turner & H.W. Reese (Eds.), *Life-span developmental psychology: Intervention* (pp. 3–28). New York: Academic Press.

Brickman, P., Kidder, L.H., Coates, D., Rabinowitz, V., Cohn, E., & Karuza, J. (1983). The dilemmas of helping: Making aid fair and effective. In J.D. Fisher, A. Nadler, & B.M. DePaulo (Eds.), *New directions in helping: Vol. 1. Recipient reactions to aid* (pp. 18–51). New York: Academic Press.

Brickman, P., Rabinowitz, V., Karuza, J., Coates, D., Cohn, E., & Kidder, L. (1982). Models of helping and coping. *American Psychologist*, *37*, 368–384.

Bronfenbrenner, U. (1975). Is early intervention effective? In B. Friedlander, G. Sterritt, & G. Kirk (Eds.), *Exceptional infant: Vol. 3. Assessment and intervention* (pp. 449–475). New York: Brunner/Mazel.

Bronfenbrenner, U. (1979). *The ecology of human development: Experiments by nature and design*. Cambridge: Harvard University Press.

Brown, I., Jr. (1979). Learned helplessness through modeling: Self-efficacy and social comparison process. In L.C. Perlmuter & R.A. Monty (Eds.), *Choice and perceived control* (pp. 107–120). Hillsdale, NJ: Lawrence Erlbaum.

Bunge, M. (1967). *Scientific research II: The search for truth*. Berlin: Springer.

Carkhuff, R.R., & Anthony, W.A. (1979). *The skills of helping*. Amherst, MA: Human Resource Development Press.

Coates, D., Renzaglia, G.J., & Embree, M.C. (1983). When helping backfires: Help and helplessness. In J.D. Fisher, A. Nadler, & B.M. DePaulo (Eds.), *New directions in helping: Vol. 1. Recipient reactions to aid* (pp. 251–279). New York: Academic Press.

Cohen, S., & Syme, S.L. (Eds.) (1985a). *Social support and health.* New York: Academic Press.

Cohen, S., & Syme, S.L. (1985b). Issues in the study and application of social support. In S. Cohen & S.L. Syme (Eds.), *Social support and health* (pp. 3–22). New York: Academic Press.

Colletta, N. (1981). Social support and the risk of maternal rejection by adolescent mothers. *The Journal of Psychology, 109,* 191–197.

Crnic, K.A., Greenberg, M.T., Ragozin, A., Robinson, N., & Basham, R. (1983). Effects of stress and social support on mothers of premature and full-term infants. *Child Development, 54,* 209–217.

Crnic, K.A., Greenberg, M.T., & Slough, N.M. (1986). Early stress and social support influences on mothers' and high-risk infants' functioning in late infancy. *Infant Mental Health Journal, 7,* 19–48.

Curran, D. (1983). *Traits of a healthy family.* Minneapolis, MN: Winston Press.

Deal, A., Trivette, C.M., & Dunst, C.J. (1987). *Styles of family functioning scale.* Unpublished scale, Family, Infant and Preschool Program, Western Carolina Center, Morganton, NC.

DePaulo, B., Nadler, A., & Fisher, J. (Eds.). (1983). *New directions in helping: Vol. 2. Help-seeking.* New York: Academic Press.

Dunst, C.J. (1985). Rethinking early intervention. *Analysis and Intervention in Developmental Disabilities, 5,* 165–201.

Dunst, C.J. (1986a). *Helping relationships and enabling and empowering families.* Paper presented at the 11th Annual Regional Intervention Program Expansion Conference, Cleveland, OH.

Dunst, C.J. (1986b). *A rating scale for assessing parent-child play opportunities.* Unpublished scale, Family, Infant and Preschool Program, Western Carolina Center, Morganton, NC.

Dunst, C.J. (1986c). *A short form scale for measuring parental health and well-being.* Unpublished manuscript, Family, Infant and Preschool Program, Western Carolina Center, Morganton, NC.

Dunst, C.J. (1986d). *Measuring parent commitment to professionally-prescribed, child-level interventions.* Unpublished manuscript, Family Infant and Preschool Program, Western Carolina Center, Morganton, NC.

Dunst, C.J., Cooper, C.S., Weeldreyer, J.C., Snyder, K.D., & Chase, J.H. (1985). *Family needs scale.* Unpublished scale, Family, Infant and Preschool Program, Western Carolina Center, Morganton, NC.

Dunst, C.J., Jenkins, V., & Trivette, C.M. (1984). Family support scale: Reliability and validity. *Journal of Individual, Family, and Community Wellness, 1,* 45–52.

Dunst, C.J., & Leet, H.E. (1987). Measuring the adequacy of resources in households with young children. *Child: Care, Health and Development, 13*, 111–125.

Dunst, C.J., Leet, H.E., Vance, S.D., & Cooper, C.S. (1986). *Resource scale for teenage mothers.* Unpublished scale, Family, Infant and Preschool Program, Western Carolina Center, Morganton, NC.

Dunst, C.J., & Trivette, C.M. (1985a). *Support functions scale: Reliability and validity.* Unpublished scale, Family, Infant and Preschool Program, Western Carolina Center, Morganton, NC.

Dunst, C.J., & Trivette, C.M. (1985b). *A guide to measures of social support and family behavior.* Monograph of Technical Assistance Development System (No. 1). Chapel Hill, NC: TADS.

Dunst, C.J., & Trivette, C.M. (1985c). *Personal time commitment scale: Reliability and validity.* Unpublished scale, Family, Infant and Preschool Program, Morganton, NC.

Dunst, C.J., & Trivette, C.M. (1987). Enabling and empowering families: Conceptual and intervention issues. *School Psychology Review, 16*(4), 443–456.

Dunst, C.J., & Trivette, C.M. (in press-a). A family systems model of early intervention with handicapped and developmentally-at-risk children. In D.P. Powell (Ed.), *Parent education and support programs: Consequences for children and families.* Norwood, NJ: Ablex Publishing.

Dunst, C.J., & Trivette, C.M. (in press-b). Toward experimental evaluation of the Family, Infant and Preschool Program. In H. Weiss & F. Jacobs (Eds.), *Evaluating family programs.* New York: Aldine Publishing.

Dunst, C.J., & Trivette, C.M. (in press-c). Helping, helplessness, and harm. In J. Witt, S. Elliott, & F. Gresham (Eds.), *Handbook of behavior therapy in education.* New York: Plenum Press.

Dunst, C.J., & Trivette, C.M. (in press-d). Assessment of family and community support. In S.J. Meisels & J.P. Shonkoff (Eds.), *Handbook of early intervention: Theory, practice and analysis.* New York: Cambridge University Press.

Dunst, C.J., Vance, S.D., & Cooper, C.S. (1986). A social systems perspective of adolescent pregnancy: Determinants of parent and parent-child behavior. *Infant Mental Health Journal, 7*, 34–48.

Fewell, R. (1986). The measurement of family functioning. In L. Bickman & D.L. Weatherford (Eds.), *Evaluating early intervention programs for severely handicapped children and their families* (pp. 263–307). Austin, TX: PRO-ED.

Fewell, R., Meyer, D.J., & Schell, G. (1981). *Parent needs inventory.* Unpublished scale, University of Washington, Seattle, WA.

Fisher, J.D. (1983). Recipient reactions to aid: The parameters of the field. In J.D. Fisher, A. Nadler, & B.M. DePaulo (Eds.), *New directions in helping: Vol. 1. Recipient reactions to aid* (pp. 3–14). New York: Academic Press.

Fisher, J.D., Nadler, A., & DePaulo, B.M. (Eds.). (1983). *New directions in helping: Vol. 1. Recipient reactions to aid.* New York: Academic Press.

Fisher, J.D., Nadler, A., & Whitcher-Alagna, S. (1983). Four theoretical approaches for conceptualizing reactions to aid. In J.D. Fisher, A. Nadler, & B.M. DePaulo (Eds.), *New directions in helping: Vol. 1. Recipient reactions to aid* (pp. 51–84). New York: Academic Press.

Folkman, S. (1984). Personal control and stress and coping processes: A theoretical analysis. *Journal of Personality and Social Psychology, 46*, 839–852.

Folkman, S., & Lazarus, R.S. (1980). An analysis of coping in a middle-aged community sample. *Journal of Health and Social Behavior, 21*, 219–239.

Folkman, S., & Lazarus, R.S. (1985). If it changes it must be a process: Study of emotion and coping during three stages of a college examination. *Journal of Personality and Social Psychology, 48*, 150–170.

Folkman, S., Lazarus, R.S., Dunkel-Shetter, C., DeLorgis, A., & Gruen, R.J. (1986). The dynamics of a stressful encounter: Cognitive appraisal, coping, and encounter outcomes. *Journal of Personality and Social Psychology, 50*, 992–1003.

Foster, M., Berger, M., & McLean, M. (1981). Rethinking a good idea: A reassessment of parent involvement. *Topics in Early Childhood Special Education, 1*(3), 55–65.

Garbarino, J. (1982). *Children and families in the social environment.* New York: Aldine Publishing.

Garrett, A. (1982). *Interviewing: Its principles and methods.* New York: Family Service Association of America.

Goldfarb, L.A., Brotherson, M.J., Summers, J.A., & Turnbull, A.P. (1986). Family needs survey. In L.A. Goldfarb, M.J. Brotherson, J.A. Summers, & A.P. Turnbull (Eds.), *Meeting the challenge of disability or chronic illness: A family guide* (pp. 77–78). Baltimore: Paul H. Brookes Publishing.

Goranson, R.E., & Berkowitz, L. (1966). Reciprocity & responsibility reactions to prior help. *Journal of Personality and Social Psychology, 3*, 227–232.

Gottlieb, B.H. (1981). Preventive interventions involving social networks and social support. In B.H. Gottlieb (Ed.), *Social networks and social support* (pp. 201–232). Beverly Hills, CA: Sage.

Gottlieb, B.H. (1983). *Social support strategies: Guidelines for mental health practice.* Beverly Hills, CA: Sage.

Greenberg, M.S., & Westcott, D.R. (1983). Indebtedness as a mediator of reactions to aid. In J.D. Fisher, A. Nadler, & B.M. DePaulo (Eds.), *New directions in helping: Vol. 1. Recipient reactions to aid* (pp. 85–112). New York: Academic Press.

Gross, A.E., & McMullen, P.A. (1983). Models of the help-seeking process. In B. DePaulo, A. Nadler, & J. Fisher (Eds.), *New directions in helping: Vol. 2. Help-seeking* (pp. 45–70). New York: Academic Press.

Gross, A.E., Wallston, B.S., & Piliavin, I. (1979). Reactance attribution, equity, and the help recipient. *Journal of Applied Social Psychology, 9*, 297–313.

Hall, A., & Wellman, B. (1985). Social networks and social support. In S. Cohen & S.L. Syme (Eds.), *Social support and health* (pp. 23–42). New York: Academic Press.

Hartman, A., & Laird, J. (1983). *Family-centered social work practice.* New York: Free Press.

Hill, R. (1971). *The strengths of black families.* New York: Emerson Hall.

Hobbs, N. (1975). *The futures of children: Categories, labels, and their consequences.* San Francisco: Jossey-Bass.

Hobbs, N., Dokecki, P.R., Hoover-Dempsey, K.V., Moroney, R.M., Shayne, M.W., & Weeks, K.H. (1984). *Strengthening families.* San Francisco: Jossey Bass.

Holroyd, J. (1985). *Questionnaire on resources and stress manual.* Unpublished scale, University of California, Neuropsychiatric Institute, Department of Psychiatric and Behavioral Sciences, Los Angeles.

House, J.S., & Kahn, R.L. (1985). Measures and concepts of social support. In S. Cohen & S.L. Syme (Eds.), *Social support and health* (pp. 83 – 108). New York: Academic Press.

Hull, C.L. (1943). *Principles of behavior.* New York: Appleton-Century-Crofts.

Kahn, R.H., Wethington, E., & Ingersoll-Dayton, B. (1987). Social support and social networks: Determinants, effects, and interactions. In R.P. Abeles (Ed.), *Life-span perspectives and social psychology.* Hillsdale, NJ: Lawrence Erlbaum Associates.

Karuza, J., Jr., Zevon, M.A., Rabinowitz, V.C., & Brickman, P. (1982). Attribution of responsibility by helpers and recipients. In T.A. Wills (Ed.), *Basic processes in helping relationships* (pp. 107 – 129). New York: Academic Press.

Langer, E.J., & Benevento, A. (1978). Self-induced dependence. *Journal of Personality and Social Psychology, 36,* 866 – 893.

Lazer, I., & Darlington, R. (1982). Lasting effects of early education: A report from the consortium for longitudinal studies. *Monographs of the Society for Research in Child Development, 47* (2 – 3, Serial No. 195).

Lewin, K. (1931). Environmental forces in child behavior and development. In C. Murchison (Ed.), *Handbook of child psychology* (pp. 94 – 127). Worcester, MA: Clark University Press.

Lewis, J.M., Beavers, W.R., Gossett, J.T., & Phillips, V.A. (1976). *No single thread: Psychological health in family systems.* New York: Brunner/Mazel.

Little, B.R. (1983). Personal projects: A rationale and method for investigation. *Environment and Behavior, 19,* 273 – 309.

Maple, F.F. (1977). *Shared decision making.* Beverly Hills, CA: Sage.

Maslow, A. (1954). *Motivation and personality.* New York: Harper & Row.

McCubbin, H.I., Comeau, J.K., & Harkins, J.A. (1981). Family inventory of resources for management. In H.I. McCubbin & J.M. Patterson (Eds.), *Systematic assessment of family stress, resources and coping* (pp. 67 – 69). St. Paul, MN: Family Stress and Coping Project.

McKillip, J. (1987). *Need analysis: Tools for the human services and education.* Beverly Hills, CA: Sage.

Merton, R.K. (1976). *Sociological ambivalence.* New York: Free Press.

Merton, V., Merton, R.K., & Barber, E. (1983). Client ambivalence in professional relationships: The problem of seeking help from strangers. In B. DePaulo, A. Nadler, & J. Fisher (Eds.), *New directions in helping: Vol. 2. Help-seeking* (pp. 13–44). New York: Academic Press.

Moore, J.A., Hamerlynck, L.A., Barsh, E.T., Spicker, S., & Jones, R.R. (1982). *Extending family resources.* Unpublished scale, Children's Clinic & Preschool, Seattle, WA.

Moos, R.H. (Ed.). (1986). *Coping with life crisis: An integrated approach.* New York: Plenum Press.

Morrison, J.K., Bushell, J.D., Hanson, G.D., Fentiman, J.R., & Holdridge-Crane, S. (1977). Relationship between psychiatric patients' attitudes toward mental illness and attitudes of dependence. *Psychological Reports, 41,* 1194.

Murray, H. (1938). *Explorations in personality.* New York: Oxford University Press.

Nadler, A., Fisher, J.D., & DePaulo, B.M. (Eds.) (1983). *New directions in helping: Vol. 3. Applied perspectives on help-seeking and -receiving.* New York: Academic Press.

Nadler, A., & Mayseless, O. (1983). Recipient self-esteem and reactions to help. In J.D. Fisher, A. Nadler, & B.M. DePaulo (Eds.), *New directions in helping: Vol. 1. Recipient reactions to aid* (pp. 167–188). New York: Academic Press.

O'Leary, A. (1985). Self-efficacy and health. *Behavior Research and Therapy, 23,* 437–451.

Olson, D.H., Larsen, A.S., & McCubbin, H.I. (1983). Family strengths. In D.H. Olson, H.I. McCubbin, H.L. Barnes, A.S. Larsen, M.L. Muxen, & M.A. Wilson (Eds.), *Families: What makes them work* (pp. 261–262). Beverly Hills, CA: Sage.

Oritt, E.C., Paul, S.C., & Behrman, J.A. (1985). The perceived support network inventory. *American Journal of Community Psychology, 13,* 565–582.

Otto, H.A. (1962). What is a strong family? *Marriage and Family Living, 24,* 77–81.

Otto, H.A. (1963). Criteria for assessing family strengths. *Family Process, 2,* 329–334.

Otto, H.A. (1975). *The use of family strength concepts and methods in family life education: A handbook.* Beverly Hills, CA: The Holistic Press.

Palys, T.S. (1980). Personal project systems and perceived life satisfaction. *Dissertation Abstracts International, 41,* 18948–18958.

Patterson, J.M., & McCubbin, H.I. (1983). Chronic illness: Family stress and coping. In C.R. Figley & H.I. McCubbin (Eds.), *Stress and the family: Vol. II. Coping with catastrophe* (pp. 21–36). New York: Brunner-Mazel.

Pattison, E.M., DeFrancisco, D., Wood, P., Frazier, H., & Crowder, J. (1975). A psychosocial kinship model for family therapy. *American Journal of Psychiatry, 132,* 1246–1251.

Pearlin, L.I., & Schooler, C. (1978). The structure of coping. *Journal of Health and Social Behavior, 19,* 2–21.

Pilisuk, M., & Parks, S.H. (1986). *The healing web: Social networks and human survival.* Hanover, NH: University Press of New England.

Rabinowitz, V.C., Karuza, J., Jr., & Zevon, M.A. (1984). Fairness and effectiveness in premeditated helping. In R. Folger (Ed.), *The sense of injustice* (pp. 63–92). New York: Plenum.

Rappaport, J. (1981). In praise of paradox: A social policy of empowerment over prevention. *American Journal of Community Psychology, 9*, 1 – 25.

Rappaport, J. (1987). Terms of empowerment/exemplars of prevention: Toward a theory for community psychology. *American Journal of Community Psychology, 15*(2), 121 – 128.

Reese, H., & Overton, W. (1980). Models of development and theories of development. In L. Goulet & P. Baltes (Eds.), *Life span developmental psychology: Research and commentary* (pp. 116 – 145). New York: Academic Press.

Reid, W.J. (1985). *Family problem solving*. New York: Columbia University Press.

Robinson, L.E., & DeRosa, S.M. (1980). *Parent Needs Inventory*. Austin, TX: Parent Consultants.

Sanders, G.F., Walters, J., & Montgomery, J.E. (1985). Family strengths of older couples and their adult children. In R. Williams, H. Lingren, G. Rowe, S. Van Zundt, P. Lee, & N. Stinnett (Eds.), *Family strengths VI: Enhancement of interaction* (pp. 85 – 97). Lincoln: College of Home Economics, University of Lincoln.

Satir, V. (1972). *Peoplemaking*. Palo Alto, CA: Science and Behavior Books.

Skinner, B.F. (1978). The ethics of helping people. In L. Wispe (Ed.) *Sympathy, altruism and helping behavior* (pp. 249 – 262). New York: Academic Press.

Slater, M.A., & Wikler, L. (1986). "Normalized" family resources for families with a developmentally disabled child. *Social Work, 31*, 385 – 390.

Snyder, K.D., Weeldreyer, J.C., Dunst, C.J., & Cooper, C.S. (1986). *Parent self-awareness scale: Reliability and validity*. Unpublished scale, Family, Infant and Preschool Program, Western Carolina Center, Morganton, NC.

Solomon, M.A. (1985). How do we really empower families? New strategies for social work practitioners. *Family Resource Coalition Report, 3*, 2 – 3.

Stevenson, P., Lee, P., Stinnett, N., & DeFrain, J. (1983). Family commitment mechanisms and family functionality. *Family Perspective, 17*, 175 – 180.

Stinnett, N. (1979). Strengthening families. *Family Perspective, 13*, 3 – 9.

Stinnett, N. (1980). Introduction. In J. DeFrain & P. Knaub (Eds.), *Family strengths: Positive models for family life* (pp. 1 – 2). Lincoln, NE: University of Nebraska Press.

Stinnett, N. (1985). Research on strong families. In G.A. Rekers (Ed.), *National leadership forum on strong families*. Ventura, CA: Regal Books.

Stinnett, N., & DeFrain, J. (Eds.) (1985a). *Secrets of strong families*. New York: Berkley Books.

Stinnett, N., & DeFrain, J. (1985b). Family Strengths Inventory. In N. Stinnett & J. DeFrain (Eds.), *Secrets of strong families* (pp. 180 – 182). New York: Berkley Books.

Stinnett, N., Knorr, B., DeFrain, J., & Rowe, G. (1981). How strong families cope with crisis. *Family Perspective, 15*(4), 159 – 166.

Stinnett, N., Lynn, D., Kimmons, L., Fuenning, S., & DeFrain, J. (1984). Family strengths and personal wellness. *Wellness Perspectives, 1*, 25 – 31.

Stinnett, N., Tucker, D.M., & Shell, D.F. (1985). Executive families: Strengths, stress, & loneliness. *Wellness Perspectives, 2*(1), 21 – 29.

Stoneman, Z. (1985). Family involvement in early childhood special education programs. In N.H. Fallen & W. Umansky (Eds.), *Young children with special needs* (2nd ed.) (pp. 442–469). Columbus, OH: Charles E. Merrill.

Summers, J.A., Turnbull, A.P., & Brotherson, M.J. (1985). *Coping strategies for families with disabled children.* Unpublished manuscript, University of Kansas, Kansas University Affiliated Facility at Lawrence.

Tardy, C.H. (1985). Social support measurement. *American Journal of Community Psychology, 13*, 187–202.

Thomas, W.I., & Thomas, D.S. (1928). *The child in America.* New York: Alfred Knopp Publishing Company.

Trivette, C.M., Deal, A., & Dunst, C.J. (1986). Family needs, sources of support, and professional roles: Critical elements of family systems assessment and intervention. *Diagnostique, 11*, 246–267.

Trivette, C.M., & Dunst, C.J. (1985). *Personal well-being index: Reliability and validity.* Unpublished scale, Family, Infant and Preschool Program, Western Carolina Center.

Trivette, C.M., & Dunst, C.J. (1986). *Inventory of social support: Reliability and validity.* Unpublished scale, Family, Infant and Preschool Program, Western Carolina Center, Morganton, NC.

Trivette, C.M., & Dunst, C.J. (1987a). *Caregiver styles of interaction: Child, parent, family, and extra-family influences.* Unpublished manuscript, Family, Infant and Preschool Program, Western Carolina Center, Morganton, NC.

Trivette, C.M., & Dunst, C.J. (1987b). *Personal network matrix.* Unpublished scale, Family, Infant and Preschool Program, Western Carolina Center, Morganton, NC.

Trivette, C.M., & Dunst, C.J. (in preparation). *Notions of constitutional support and its relationship to maternal well-being.*

Turner, R.J. (1983). Direct, indirect, and moderating effects of social support on psychological distress and associated conditions. In H.B. Kaplan (Ed.), *Psychological stress: Trends in theory and research* (pp, 105–155). New York: Academic Press.

Wikler, L., & Keenan, M. (Eds.). (1983). *Developmental disabilities: No longer a private tragedy.* Silver Spring, MD and Washington, DC: NASW and AAMD.

Williams, R., Lindgren, H., Rowe, G., Van Zandt, S., & Stinnett, N. (Eds.). (1985). *Family strengths 6: Enhancement of interaction.* Lincoln, NE: Department of Human Development and the Family, Center for Family Strengths, University of Nebraska.

Zigler, E., & Berman, W. (1983). Discerning the future of early childhood intervention. *American Psychologist, 38*, 894–906.

Author Index

Subject Index